The Mourning After:
A Journey Through
Death, Grief, and Healing

The Mourning After: A Journey Through Death, Grief, and Healing

Darcy Donovan

Darcy Donovan
Copyright © 2014

Copyright © 2014 by Darcy Donovan

All rights reserved. This book or any portion thereof may not be reproduced or used in any manner whatsoever without the express written permission of the publisher except for the use of brief quotations in a book review or scholarly journal.

This book is based on actual events. At the author's discretion, some names and places have been changed.

First Printing: December, 2014

ISBN 978-0-9940029-0-7

Visit the website:

www.TheMourningAfter.ca

Dedication

Dedicated to my parents:
Rose and James Donovan.
Thank you, mom and dad,
for everything.

Contents

Pre-Dawn 1
The Presentation 13
    Disclosure 15
    My Father 16
    January 29-30, 2010 21
    Aftermath 25
    Therapy 41
    Strange Things Will Happen 69
    Questions 75
After The Mourning After
    My Dad's Eulogy 87
    When Does It Stop Hurting So Much? 95
    Ceilidh Surprise 99
    Good Bye, Irene 111
    The Lost Cherubs 117
    My Perfect House 125
    Renovated 145
    Sunset 155
    No Regrets 161

About the Book Cover

In case you were ever curious, yes, that is me walking away on the cover of the book. The path is a beautiful hiking trail at Nicolle Flats in Saskatchewan, Canada. It is near where my father's ashes were spread.

The visage in the clouds is a stylized version of one of the last photos of my father. Even though he no longer walks these trails, his presence abides.

☙

Pre-Dawn

The Eulogy

"Alright," I whispered to my mom as I tapped her on the knee, "Here goes nothing." I got up from the front-row pew and approached the podium. It was time for my dad's eulogy.

My mom and I were still numb from the events of past 7 days. Heck, there was a haze from the previous month as, 27 days earlier, we had lost my Uncle Dave – my mom's brother – in almost the same fashion. For us, it was like successive earthquakes; the first that rattles close to home and weakens the foundation; the next that finds you right on the fault line and swallows you whole. We were still on our backs in the crater that was our Ground Zero.

"I'm here! I'm here! Oh glory be!" I bellowed, mimicking my father as I adjusted the microphone, "This is what I'm sure my dad said when he first arrived in heaven. Dad was one to pull out such...*unique* phrases."

I was standing before an audience of friends, family, and foes. You could have interchanged "family" and "foe" almost at will this day as, in the congregation, sat two of my sisters who had abandoned my father shortly after his cancer diagnosis 15 months ago. They had their convoluted reasons I am sure, but I couldn't excuse how they walked away from a parent – a *good* parent! – in a time of need. They had issues that would become abundantly clear a month after the funeral as one of them fell victim to domestic violence and an ugly divorce that required multiple interventions from police and the courts. Was the other trapped in a similar situation?

In my mind, their respective personal tumults didn't justify abandoning their father when he was at his most vulnerable. However, I wasn't in their shoes and didn't see their justifications. Regardless of their logic, I was thankful I didn't have to face the person that looked back at them in the mirror. On this, the day of the funeral, I had no foreknowledge of what was about to happen to one of them. Despite my anger and contempt for them on this day, I would experience no pleasure or vindication when I would hear the news of the domestic abuse three months later. Why would I?

There was no way around it; this was a lose/lose situation.

This eulogy was, in part, directed at them. It wasn't an angry spit in their direction; it was intended to be a review of what they missed in the last year of my dad's life. To me, spending time with my dad as he straddled fighting for his life while preparing for a possible exit was a beautiful journey. It was something I considered a farewell gift he could have given to all his children had they put down their shields, swords, and spears.

"Even as I watched dad physically reduce before my eyes over the next 15 months," I said to the congregation, "I discovered this man of inner strength and determination."

I was emboldened this day. A week earlier, I witnessed an indignity to a dignified man that cost him his life and I had to do something to right a wrong. This was a mission! I am a seasoned public speaker, but never was it more important than now. I had made a promise to my father as he lay in that bed, comatose from a medical mistake that was zealously covered up before my eyes. I was told lies I was supposed to believe like the dumb commoner I am, even though I saw quite the opposite. *Trust us*, was the overall message, *we are medical professionals who are better than you; we don't make mistakes*. I would hold my dad's hand unto his final moments and said I was going to do the eulogy for him. I promised I would somehow right this.

I would right this. I promise.

This was my frame of mind the week leading up to the funeral. This eulogy had to be perfect. It had to tell a story and it had to send a message. It was not going to list a series of milestones like a resume and offer pedestrian platitudes. The goal was to not only tell the story of my father; it was to bring people into the most formative and influential contact in our life; the parent-child relationship.

And it worked.

After the service, I had many people come up to me who wanted to talk about the eulogy. Many told me it was one of the best they'd ever heard. I thought it was a polite thing to say because, don't we all say that in the emotional tidal wave of a funeral service? The compliments didn't resonate until the funeral director told me that it stood out from all the ones he'd witnessed. Now *that* was an objective compliment!

Of course, there were detractors. When my wayward sisters were approached on the matter, one of them replied, "Sure it was good...if you like made up stories." The irony of such a statement from an absentee sibling was not lost on me. Especially when the totality of their support was to come to the hospital in the final hours just to watch my father die. How could they possibly discern truth from untruth from the safety and comfort of their living room while my parent's world burned to the ground?

Other people would be more charitable.

"That was so…how you spoke of the relationship with your dad was just…" said an elderly man who came up to me, his bottom lip tremored as he fought to find the words, "I have three daughters and…" He trailed off as words eluded him and he looked away. He didn't have to say another word. He was thinking about the relationship he had with his children. He was thinking about the world he had built for them and with them, and if it had been worth it. For certain it was worth it for him. But, for a moment, there seemed to be a creeping doubt as he looked down. Was he a good dad? Did he honour his children so that they, in turn, would honour him?

I saw these things stir inside of him and recognized the need to quell his doubts. I reached out, touched his arm and said, "Thank you." I gave him a look that was supposed to say, *you are a good dad, I can tell.* He nodded and shook himself out of the moment because men from his era aren't supposed to show weakness. He gave a weak smile, nodded again and walked away. He wanted to say more but his words were congested in a narrow egress.

This was exactly what I wanted to convey. This funeral wasn't just about my father; it was about all of us and our relationships with each other. My dad was a humble man and likely would have been uncomfortable with an event being all about him. Early in my dad's life, he was an educator and it was important to him that other people learn something. His memorial would provide the opportunity for one more lesson; one more opportunity to learn.

After the funeral, I had considered the matter complete. I didn't think I would get the chance to talk about this again in a public forum. I had shaken the dust off my feet and prepared to move on with my life even though what lurked around the corner was a year-long storm that would strip me of most everything in my life.

For three and a half years, I would hear the odd story of the eulogy and how it had been reprinted and passed around. The local Knights of Columbus would make mention of it in a meeting. Distant relatives of my father in Ontario wanted copies of it. The odd person at a family event would tell me about it. Even though years would pass, it kept making its rounds. I thought it was a novelty that would run its course.

The Invitation

"Happy Easter! How are things going in your life? I hope that you are well." read the email from my friend Crystal, "In May we are hosting a Grief Seminar and I am wondering if you would like to share your story of loss and healing with the group that evening. We are having two other speakers share their stories. Your presentation would be allotted 20 minutes."

Crystal is a good friend of mine who happens to be an after care facilitator at a funeral home. She is one of the gentlest spirits I know and is everything I am not when it comes to being calm and to listen. I relied on her many times after my father's passing if only just to talk to someone. She always was understanding and had great insights into the nature of grief and healing. Crystal is perfect for her job and I can't imagine too many people that are better than her at that profession. "Take the gentle path" is her mantra and I admire that she walks her talk.

I was honoured by Crystal's decision to invite me to speak at her event. I asked why and she said that, after witnessing the eulogy I gave for my father, that I would be a good candidate to share my story on death, grief, and healing. Crystal said that it is a difficult subject for many people and very few are ever willing to step up and share their story. She said that it is important for some people to share, and it is also important for some people to listen and discover that they are not alone on this journey; that there are many people out there who go through the same range of emotions. Sometimes, all people really need to know is that they aren't alone, that their struggle isn't unique, and that there is a time on the other side of grief when things get better. Who better to talk about something like this than someone who's been there?

The opportunity was one that I couldn't resist. I had been through a firestorm after my father's passing and I had given friends advice on the do's and don't's of handling an estate since I made many mistakes and endured a world of punishment. I would refer to that year after my dad's death as my own personal fire walk. I joked that if you ever want a measure of revenge against your enemies after you die, then make them the executor of your estate. I thought a first-hand account of my experience would serve as a good warning to others. Maybe it would even make some people thankful that they weren't me!

My biggest challenge to writing the speech was that I had only 20 minutes. At first I thought this would be plenty of time, but once I started to dig into my story and the range of emotions I had, 20 minutes was only going to cover one portion of story. I could have given 20 minutes on anger, 20 minutes on resentment, 20 minutes on family issues and the list grew with each new thought. How was I going to fit this all into 20 minutes?

I did manage to put together a multimedia presentation within the allotted 20 minute timeline, but it only felt like a quick kiss into the nature of death, grief, and healing. I went back and forth on a particular story that might put me out there as someone who is crazy. I would put the story in, then take it out, and then put it back in again. Should I tell this? Or, shouldn't I?

It was the telepathic "I'm okay" experience I had about an hour after my father's passing.

I believe my dad did give me a message shortly after he died to let me know that he's okay and his spirit had a safe crossover into eternity. But, those are my personal beliefs that may not stand up to scrutiny because they can't be reproduced in a lab. I understand that there are ways to explain this away as some sort of self-deception; a method my psyche used to protect itself from immense pain in the same manner a blister forms on a burn.

My argument against this being a self-deception is that the moment would send me into a deep depression because, while I got a wonderful message that should have appeased me, I was not allowed to go with it. It felt like my dad had gone to a wonderful place where there is nothing but the purest form of love and I was left behind. If this was a form of psychological self-protection, it could be argued that this particular method backfired.

Further to my thoughts against it being a self-deception is, while I was in a deep depression afterwards, I never lost the desire to live because I did not want to disappoint this loving entity and give account for a self-scripted exit. It felt far worse than anything in this life to feel disappointment coming from it and have it ask, *"Why did you do that?"* It is not that I was afraid of being smote with anger; the disappointment *was* the punishment.

It was, as I say in the presentation, a bitter-sweet moment of beauty, poetry and perfection that has yet to be duplicated in my life before or since that day. It was also a moment that I never spoke of for almost two years because it was deeply personal, and also, talking about it potentially exposed me to a type of "pearls before swine" ridicule. This was the stuff of Hollywood fantasy, right? Suspend your disbelief until the credits roll and then back to reality…right?

As far as I was concerned, that *was* reality.

After debating this part of the presentation, I finally just cast caution to the wind and decided to put it in and leave it in. I felt that "I'm okay" is the ultimate message in this presentation whether you believe that moment was real or delusory. I thought that if I survived all of this, and if I'm okay, then so shall you be.

The Presentation

It would be a wonderful night of sharing. I met the other two presenters; one lost a brother to a murder that had left her open to the wolf pack of the media and the other lost a teen daughter to a car accident just before high school graduation. When it came to my turn, I wasn't nervous as I gave the presentation. I was emboldened in the same way I was the day of my dad's eulogy. *Make it about them and not you,* I thought as I stepped up to the podium. I delivered my 20 minute speech, dusted off my hands and thought that would be it.

I was wrong.

I had a constant lineup of 5 and 6 people deep wanting to talk to me during intermission. I was not expecting this at all. People told me they could relate to things like my bitterness towards Canadian health "care" and the lack of help from my siblings. It seemed sad that my story wasn't unique and, sadder still that the world is not lacking when it comes to disgrace. The part that didn't surprise me was that the "I'm okay" story had particularly touched a nerve and people wanted to share their experiences of possible contact after a death. Every one of them had been too afraid to talk about it and found a safe harbour once it was mentioned. I was privy to some great and wonderful stories that night.

"The Mourning After"

The experience of sharing a journey through death, grief, healing inspired me to write this book. It also inspired me to expand the presentation to the lengths that I dared take it. While our stories of loss vary and are unique, the emotional landscape we traverse in the aftermath is where we find common ground. Some of what is said in this book will resonate with you; some of it will not. This book never promises to have all the answers you seek, but maybe – just maybe – it will give you some ideas on how to come to terms with your loss. There is no "one size fits all" method and, when you think about it, that would be very boring, wouldn't it? The journey is a gift and an opportunity to learn about yourself. It is designed so that you come to an understanding of why you are here.

For you who sought this book because you miss someone dear: I am sorry for your loss, and may the words that follow help you come to terms with the things you cannot change.

଼

The Presentation

Disclosure

In the interest of disclosure, I must disclose that I am a believer in God and, some of the things I say will come from that perspective. I caution that, while I consider myself a man of faith, I am not necessarily a man of religion. And, I want this distinction noted. Because, I don't necessarily come at this from a religious point of view and I don't want to speak on behalf of any denomination because I am not qualified.

If you are an agnostic or an atheist, there is still going to be some practical advice here that follows accepted psychology and will be of use to you. I'm also going to be throwing in some personal theories, so be sure to consider the source before accepting or rejecting them.

Lastly, I caution that parts of this presentation are rather raw and honest. There may be some things that I say that may offend if they are taken out of context. I would like you to indulge me and please consider the context of some of the things I say before offering a judgment on them.

With all that said, let's go!

My Father

My dad is James Donovan. He was an agrologist with Saskatchewan Agriculture and Food for much of his career. He was married for over 4 decades to his wife and my mother, Rose, and they had 5 children. I happen to be the youngest of those 5.

My dad was a good man who lived in an era where men never cry and they never show their emotions. They had to be tough, stoic and, above all, the rock of the family. And, in those ways, my dad fulfilled all of those things. He was a good provider and always taught us that we had to work for things. He reminded us that nothing in this life is given to you and, if it is, it likely isn't worth much because, easy come, and easy go.

The Relationship

Because my father was stoic, he held his cards close to his chest and he never really let you inside. It's just who he was; there's no right or wrong here.

Like any father, dad had lame catch phrases that I think were designed to drive me insane. For instance, it wasn't "chit chat"; it was "Chitty Chatty". It wasn't a "Minute"; it was a "Minootie". It wasn't a "Credit Union"; it was a "Credit Onion". Ah ha ha...yeah dad, that's funny. Now excuse me while I go hang out with my cool friends before I rip out my hair.

On the closeness scale of things, I was not on the same page as my father for the first 37 years of my life. We had different interests and different ways of expressing ourselves. There was still a deep love between us; we were just two different people who couldn't connect properly.

That is, until his diagnosis.

The Diagnosis

In the fall of 2008, my father was diagnosed with esophageal cancer. When he was first diagnosed, it was at stage one and entirely savable. However, there was only one doctor who could perform the surgery here in Regina and that surgeon was on vacation at the time. The system was unable – or unwilling – to get my father help in another city or another province.

By the time the doctor returned from vacation to *finally* perform the surgery, the cancer had spread and would be late stage 3 and almost too late. My dad had an uphill battle to begin with and, this made for an even steeper climb.

And so started my bitterness with the system.

The Caregiver Role

Over the course of the next 15 months, my father's condition would require more and more attention. I saw a hero in all of this; my mom.

You know that vow you take when you get married about "in sickness and in health", "in good times and in bad"? Well, this was the sick times and, by association, the bad times. She was true to her vows and was the most dedicated person I've ever seen. She did what I considered above and beyond the call of duty for her husband.

In light of this, after my mom had hurt her back picking up my father after he had stumbled and fell, I decided to make a huge decision; I would take a leave of absence from my job in order to help out. My compassionate leave would eventually run out and, I was faced with the prospect of resigning. I shrugged, "It's just a job. There are many others out there."

I assured dad that he helped me back in the days when I first ventured out on my own and, I was just returning the favour. Besides, I had an emergency fund for such an occasion! I will be fine! Once I explained this, it made it easier for him to accept my decision. But, he still was not comfortable with it.

The life lesson here is: It's easier to do the right thing if you have an emergency fund. I am no hero; just a good planner.

The Closed Book Opens

I've heard a great line about how, in life, you spend a good portion of it accumulating things and, towards the twilight years and into our sunset, we start to surrender everything we have acquired. In the case of my dad, he had hoarded his emotions in a tightly closed book. And, his condition forced him to open up and release all these emotions he had been hoarding.

As this closed book opened, I discovered this man of inner strength and determination. We had many talks and, for a change, each of us seemed to take interest in the other's interests. Imagine that! Our relationship changed in a way that felt like I was just starting to get to know this once tightly closed book.

One of dad's most precious physical possessions was given away just before he passed.

My grandfather had an Irish Claddagh ring. He gave it to my dad when he had just hours to live. And, my father, in turn, gave it to me as his health began to fail and he started to lose hope. It was one of those symbolic gestures that, while wonderful, came with a hanging dark cloud. I remember, when he gave it to me, how I felt a great honour and sadness in equal measure. It was a somber passing of the torch from failing hands.

Living with Cancer

Dad outlived not one, not two, but four death sentences. He far outlived most predictions and this is a testament to his healthy living and fortitude. His cancer was supposed to have taken his life much, much earlier and, was, in fact, starting to miraculously recede. There were glimpses of hope that he might actually beat this...

    That is, until January 29th, 2010.

January 29-30, 2010

It is the day that still haunts me. I wheeled my father into the hospital that morning. He was supposed to go in for a simple procedure that was supposed to take 15-20 minutes.

Well...it didn't turn out that way. Somewhere along the way, an infection was released into my father's body. I know what really happened, but I won't go into details here.

The day would take twists and turns of a situation that was falling apart. I would see and experience things that still haunt me to this day.

This mad roller coaster would go on all afternoon and into the night; He was stable...then he wasn't. He was stable again, then he wasn't...

Late in the evening, when they had stabilized my dad for what would be the last time, we had our final exchange;

"Dad? You have to stop scaring me, okay?"

"Okay...I'll stop..."

My dad would be true to his word as, shortly thereafter, he would take a final plunge and become comatose. It is then that, I would have a one way conversation with my father as he waited to exit from this life:

"I Came To Say Farewell…"

"Dad? I came to say farewell. For now. But, just for now. I want to say thank you for everything. Especially these past 15 months. You know, I've been wondering what purpose it served to have a man be perfectly healthy for the first 72 years of his life, only to have a disease take him in his 73rd. Well, dad, although the purpose is different for everyone, I think I found the purpose in all of this for me.

"I got to see a side of you I never saw before. You know how a child first sees his dad as infallible? And, then, in their teen years, all that admiration is washed away and the parent now does *nothing* right and the child wonders how in the world they could be related to them. And, then, later on, it comes to a balance.

"Well, dad, these past 15 months went deeper than just that. I got to see you not only through the eyes of a son. I got to see you through the eyes of your siblings. I got to see you through the eyes of your childhood friends. I saw you with the same vulnerabilities in your youth as I did. But, I also saw you with the same youthful dreams and aspirations…like I did. You showed me that you won some and you showed me that you lost some. You let me see the moments of heartbreak in your life. But, you also showed me more than enough that your heart can be fulfilled. And, you have with mom. I mean, your heart was so full of love for her that it was like a balloon about to burst.

"And, all those times when you had your chemo treatments. And, you looked up at me with those bright blue eyes and smiled when I arrived; you emanated an unconditional love that only a parent could give. I could feel that!

"You let me see all of this in yourself in the past year.

"Most of all, dad, you let me see that you were, indeed, human. And, you have given me the permission to be human myself; a perfectly, imperfect human being who is forever changed by you and these last 15 months. I will never be the same again because of the time I got to spend with you in the past year and a bit. You have facilitated the birth of a whole new person and I am happy with what you created in me.

"While it's hard to let you go, I would not trade the experience of walking with you on this final journey. We were shoulder to shoulder and we fought this one hard. You are, and ever shall be, my Winston Churchill who never surrendered. Even into your last and finest hour.

"We'll meet again. And, when we do, tell you what; if there is a Credit Onion in heaven, we can meet there first and we can *Chitty Chatty* for a *minootie* again like we used to. And, this one time only, I'll let *YOU* buy lunch! You don't have to worry about me stealing the bill and paying behind your back. Okay? God Bless you, Dad. We love you."

January 30, 2010

We would decide to take him off life support the next morning. Dad would pass away peacefully on January 30, 2010.

All because of a simple 15-20 minute procedure. In and out, just like that! No biggie. No biggie...

In my opinion, my dad died under a veil of suspicion, and in my opinion, what appeared to be lies. I could be wrong but, I don't think I am. It made me bitter and angry for a long time.

Aftermath

When a loved one passes, you get this punch deep in your chest. And, that punch removes a part of you and never gives it back. It changes you forever and, you'll never be the same person again. But, you'll come to realize, that this isn't a bad thing.

You see, with all the emotions you experience in the wake of a passing, the worst thing you can do to yourself is to run away and hide from those emotions. And, no kidding here, there's going to be a lot of bad emotions during this time! But, the thing you need to do is, you need to face them and embrace them. And, I know that that's a hard thing to do. Along with embracing the emotions, you need to embrace the meaning that is beneath them all.

The number one thing you will discover in all the emotions you have in the wake of a death is that they all have a basis in love; every single one of them. And, that is a not a bad thing at all! Love is not a bad thing.

What you are actually grieving is that the love you are sending out there is not coming back to you. Or, so it seems.

I'm going try to do my best to show you later that this love *IS* returning to you but, not in a way that you normally recognize. Just like the one that has passed, it has changed form.

As for me and how my dad died, I was left with many levels of anger, bitterness, guilt and depression. I was also left with a multitude of triggers and anchors.

Triggers & Anchors

What are triggers and anchors? Triggers, as you might expect, are mostly negative associations you have made with objects, sounds, smells, and certain places; anything that, for no reason, sets you off on into an extreme reaction. They come from the part of your brain called the amygdala. The amygdala is where your brain stores traumatic or threatening experiences, and it sends a warning when it perceives the same situation. This is all done to protect you; it is not meant to mess with your head by giving you a bouquet of phobias. It is a primal form of protection, and most of the time it is beneficial because it is designed to keep you alive and in one piece.

For example: if someone has an irrational fear of dogs, it could be because they felt threatened, or were legitimately attacked by one as a child. Think about it from the child's perspective; there are many dogs that are larger than you at that age and a bark can be as powerful as the roar of a dragon. That experience is stored in the amygdala and, anytime that child came into contact with a dog, the amygdala activated a visceral warning; usually manifested in a self-hug and a scream. Even though the child grows into a mature adult and can handle just about any dog, that person's brain still perceives *every* dog as the threat of that roaring dragon and it evokes the "flight or fight" response.

I had many of these after my dad's death. One of them was the mere ringing of a phone. It would instantly tighten my chest and put in me in "fight or flight" mode. It was all because most every phone call I handled was an aggressive bill collector. And, a lot of times, it resulted in a shouting match that would emotionally drain me for the rest of the day...and maybe the next.

Anchors, to me, are physical places that have an assigned meaning to you. Some of them are good; some of them are bad. As you might expect, the hospital was a bad anchor. Merely driving past the hospital and seeing it peak above the treetops would, again, make me tense up and go into "Fight or Flight". It was the Big Barking Dog.

Another bad anchor for me occurs every January 29th. Without fail, when the clock reaches 3:55pm, my breathing becomes quick and shallow. In case you are wondering, that is the exact time when the "code blue" was called and everything on that day went sideways.

Not every trigger and anchor is bad; I have a good anchor as well. It is the place where my dad's ashes were spread. I will be talking about that later and why it's a good place. This is an anchor I opt to keep.

How do you handle the bad triggers? Now that you know how your brain processes this situation, you now have to figure out how to retrain it and show that the threat or trauma is not the same as it was on that one infamous day. This means you have to confront the trigger when it happens and diminish its power. It all goes back to the recurring theme of "face and embrace".

Triggers seem to be amorphous, having no shape or presence. So, what I did is I *gave* it shape and presence. I imagined each trigger as this obnoxious person who was mocking me, and if I reacted badly, it was a precious gift to him that only made him stronger. The more I started to imagine it in that way, the more I didn't want to satisfy him because I also viewed this person as beneath me. Eventually, the power these triggers had over me became less and less. It took some time, but I started building momentum to the point where I was winning more than I lost. I still lose every now and again, but it's not as often. I can't let that obnoxious "person" win!

If you are at a loss with your own personal triggers, give that a try. What have you got to lose?

Resentment – Health Care

In addition to triggers and anchors, I had multiple levels of bitterness and resentment.

The first level of bitterness and resentment was the medical staff at the hospital. It was not *that* my dad passed, it was *how* he passed. I won't go into the details but, ultimately, what I witnessed made me lose faith in the system. It's hard when you lose trust in a place that you should be able to trust.

If you will indulge me for a moment, I must step upon a soap box:

I cringe every time I hear a fellow Canadian boast about our "free" health care and scoff at other systems; especially the Americans. Canadians have bought into a feel-good myth that gives a false sense of security and superiority. We have a pride in our freedom of choice in every aspect of our lives…except when it comes to our monopolistic "one size fits all" health care system. Our only "freedom of choice" in Canadian health care is that we have the freedom to get in line and hope we don't die before it's our turn.

But remember; it's *"free"*!

First of all, socialized health care isn't free because the deductions on my paycheque tell me it isn't free. If our health care is indeed free, then one has to assume all the infrastructure – the hospital buildings, emergency vehicles et al – was built at no cost and the all the staff perform voluntary services. The last time I checked, hospitals were built and maintained by people who were rightfully paid for their services. The last time I checked, nurses, doctors and ancillary staff also received deserving payment for their services. This leads me to the irrevocable fact that Canadian health care is *not* free.

I have heard anecdotally that the average Canadian cancer patient spends $75,000 out of pocket over their course of their illness. I believe this because my father spent in the range of $50,000 during his treatments (this includes gas, lodging and medications not covered). I have also witnessed a desperate young mother with advanced breast cancer being forced to raise and spend over $250,000 so she could go to an American clinic because the "free" Canadian system was unable to help her. I have seen people with Lyme disease who were abandoned by the "free" Canadian system and they, again, had to raise money to seek user pay help in the United States.

But remember, the Canadian system is *"free"!*

Second, from what I have witnessed, Canadian health care is a great system…as long as you don't grow old…or get sick. It's a fantastic system for your basic needs like broken limbs or emergency revival; just like every other system in the Western World. However, I am noticing a disturbing trend of the system casting off the elderly and treating them more as a nuisance than as someone who has contributed into the system their entire life. Shouldn't they be getting what they paid for?

Or, because it's "free", are they getting *exactly* what they paid for?

I am merely relaying my experience with the system. Perhaps my personal experience is unique and an anomaly. Maybe your experiences were great and, if that's the case, then I am happy for you. Feel free to disagree with me for questioning all that is sacred in Canada. But beware; maybe you will be like one of my friends who didn't believe me until their parent took ill, and I received an infamous text that said; "I now know what you mean."

Resentment – The Law

The second level of resentment was directed at the legal system. I had inquired about filing a wrongful death lawsuit. However, I was *gently* told that, such cases are rarely won followed by a bunch of legal *"bla bla bla"* that was intended to drown me in a pool of big words and make me give up.

It worked because I didn't have the energy to pursue this. I left it die on the vine. Sometimes, I wonder if I should have. However, reality keeps tapping me on the shoulder and reminding me of the Goliath I was intending to challenge. Unless I had something that was considered a "slam dunk", the odds of winning were negligible and any miraculous victory was going to be pyrrhic at best.

It took very little research to discover the chances of successful litigation in Canada for malpractice are less than 2%. According to the book *"After the Error: Speaking Out About Patient Safety to Save Lives"* by Susan McIver and Robin Wyndham, from 2005 to 2010, there were 4,524 lawsuits filed against Canadian doctors. During that five-year period, 3,089 claims were dismissed or abandoned because the court dismissed the claim or the plaintiff quit, ran out of money or died before trial. Of the 521 cases that went to trial, only 116 led to a judgment that favoured the patient. The median damage awarded was just $117,000. Keep in mind that the awarded monies do not include legal fees and expenses.

Also note that these numbers do not include people like myself who were turned away at the door of a lawyer's office in the first place. The percent chance of winning a malpractice suit in Canada might actually be less than 1%. Our system seems to be set up for impunity and unaccountability.

The worst part was that, while a win might be expensive, a loss would mean financial obliteration. Should you make it to court and likely lose the case, you are now at the mercy of the doctor's insurance company – a company with assets approaching 3 *billion* dollars – whose job it is to make you an example and a warning to others. They will sue you with almost 100% success for their legal costs. Suing for malpractice in Canada is clearly an "all or nothing" proposition designed to intimidate people into silence.

This goes back to the real reason the lawyer didn't take our case; he was too afraid of being steamrolled because he knew the deck was impossibly stacked against us.

However, I was free to brag to the world about how great our *"free"* health care system is. That was the thing I could do without consequence.

It seems our job as Canadians is to be the complacent, polite, and repeat the sacred creed about *"free"* health care. Those flaws in the system that stare us in the face? We cover our ears and sing "Mary Had a Little Lamb" at full volume to drown out the truth.

Canadians are far too comfortable saying, "I don't see the elephant the room, do you?"

Resentment – Insurance

The third level of resentment came at the expense of my father. Shortly after his passing, we discovered a nightmare scenario; my dad, in secret, cancelled his insurance plan in an attempt to get a better one. My mom was left with nothing to cover all the medical expenses that accumulated while he was sick.

What *the hell* was he thinking? Believe it or not, this is a common and frightening phenomenon. Often, one feels guilty about not leaving behind enough money and, in an irrational and desperate move, they attempt to get more. Of course, the insurance companies are more than willing to oblige and cancel it...and reassess, and reject, a dying client.

Because of all this, my mom lost just about everything and was left vulnerable and compromised.

All I can say about this is that, in the case of my dad, morphine makes you do funny, funny things.

There is an important life lesson here: if you have a loved one who is terminal and is using medications that cloud their judgement, wrestle their insurance away from them. Or, better yet, have two people on the insurance in the first place so that one can't cancel without the consent of the other. It may cause strife in your family but it is a necessary protection for those left behind.

Survivor's Guilt

As far as guilt is concerned, despite the anger towards my father, I had an indirect form of survivor's guilt. I felt guilty for wheeling my dad into the hospital that day. I felt like I had led him to his death by wheeling him into the coliseum for the lions to devour.

Somehow, I held myself to account for not possessing psychic powers. Somehow, I had these expectations of myself to know the future and avoid it. I lived with the guilt of not having a superpower for a long, long time.

I know it doesn't make sense but, when you are the one who takes someone to a place where they end up being irreparably harmed, you tend to hold yourself accountable. It doesn't matter if it makes sense or not.

The only thing that cured this line of thought was time. I just needed time to process it and replay the event over and over until all the alternate scenarios were exhausted. It was only when I came to the conclusion that I needed an impossible power that I could be absolved of the guilt.

When we are in an irrational mode like that, it is pointless for others to point out the flaws in the logic. If someone around you exhibits an irrational guilt, the only thing you can do is ask, "Do you truly believe that?" and leave the rest of the processing up to them. Remember that you can only lead them to a rational conclusion; you can't force them to accept it. Never tell anyone what they *should* be feeling or thinking; let them arrive at that on their own.

Yes, it requires patience.

Resentment – The Siblings

The last level of resentment is towards my siblings. They left me to handle all of the heavy lifting – the care giving, the chemo appointments, the estate, investigating the death, etc. – they left that all up to me.

I have 4 siblings. While *only two of them* did help here and there, they mostly left everything else in my hands. I am sure their line of thinking was, *"You're single and have no kids. You can handle it. You have the time."*

Let me tell you something about the single person with no kids; they have no support at home and, when they make mistakes, there is no safety net and there is nobody close enough for them to talk to. A married person with kids, while those people in their family require maintenance and time, still offer support and a distraction that single people do not have.

I resented all my siblings because *they* got to heal and *they* got to move on. What *they* left for me to handle required the strength of Atlas to hold up the entire world.

Well, the world eventually pancaked me. I am no Atlas.

The "Favoured One"

Not only did my siblings and their spouses leave me to handle most everything, some decided to openly mock me for doing so.

My mom often speaks highly of me for doing all that I've done. To me, this is embarrassing because, I did what you *should* do! It shouldn't warrant special praise. It would be like a boss giving praise to their employee for showing up to work on time.

My mom's praise rubbed a brother in law the wrong way. He mocked me behind my back, referring to me as "The Favoured One".

The Favoured One?!

Seriously? He infers that I made all these sacrifices for the glorification of self. I put my career in jeopardy, quit my job, and became a caregiver. Then, I became an executor who fought with collectors every day for a year.

When you add up all the losses, it totals tens of thousands of dollars in lost wages and emotional tolls that still show their scars to this day. This is what you get in exchange for the ceremonial title of "The Favoured One".

Gee, where does one sign up?

In the interest of equal time, please allow me to bestow a title upon that person; "Observer"; "Spectator"; "Bystander".

Not the title you were thinking I'd choose, now was it?

I realize that neither of the titles are flattering but, when you think about it, if you had a choice, which title would you rather have? At least, with "The Favoured One", there is an assumption that you did *something*.

If, at the end of my life, there is a Judgment Seat, and if I have to stand before The Almighty and give account for the things I have or have not done, when it comes to my father and my parents in general, I can admit that, although I failed them innumerable times in my life, I stepped up when they needed me the most; for the most critical times in their lives when they needed someone to stand with them, at least I can say that I was there.

My siblings cannot say the same.

What do you think my siblings see when they look themselves in the mirror? If they had to stand before a Judgment Seat to give account, what do you think they would say?

To be honest with you, I don't envy them.

Relationship with the Siblings, Present Day

To this day, I cannot say that I have a strong relationship with my siblings, and I don't know if that will ever be repaired. It could be irreconcilable. After much consideration, I have come to terms with and am okay with that. I don't need impostors in my life – and neither do you! It shouldn't matter who it is.

The blood relations in your life are people who, in my opinion, are there by accident of birth. They do not have a special privilege bestowed upon them to take advantage of you. While you cannot choose your blood relatives, you can choose who your inner circle is. Relatives are the most likely candidates to hurt you the most and you should harbour no guilt for omitting anyone – bloodline or not – who does not have your best interests at heart.

Struggles to Forgive

The thing that I do need to do, though, is I need to forgive. One thing that I am figuring out, in the case of my siblings and their spouses, is that they are projecting their guilt for their lack of action onto me. In a strange way, it's nothing personal; I'm just a big movie screen for which to project their own shortcomings; a scapegoat for their own sins, as it were.

When it comes to a lot of these situations, it's not about you; it's about them. You just happen to be an instrument. You are simply making them feel better about themselves as they sacrifice you on the altar of their narrow mind. There is nothing you can do about it.

Speaking of people who say thoughtless things, have you been told to "get over it"? Have you had people try to "fix" you with quick solutions? And, then, when you didn't "get over it" in the timeframe that was convenient for them, they get mad at you? Well, that's because they couldn't take credit for fixing you. They were frustrated and, took their personal "failure" out on you.

If you can see that it's actually not about you, it might be easier to forgive them. Maybe! Forgiveness is a hard thing to manifest when the other party isn't aware and isn't sorry.

As for forgiveness, I've not done that yet. I am still coming to terms with what it means. I am still wrestling with the idea that forgiveness does *not* equate to condoning their actions. It does *not* mean that I forget the wrongs. It does *not* mean that I welcome them back into my life. It just means that I forgive them and let go of the anger if only for my sake.

While we are at it, I need to forgive that doctor, those nurses, that lawyer, and those collection agents. I need to forgive them all.

So, I am here, writing this as a hypocrite and saying that, for those who have wronged you during your time of grief, you will need to forgive them. If you don't, it will do more harm to you than it will to them. Rest assured, your bitterness towards them isn't changing the way they brush their teeth in the morning. The acid you pour upon yourself in order to "teach them a lesson" is going unnoticed while it's burning a hole in you.

So, do as I say and not as I do; forgive them...for you.

Therapy

When it comes to our healing journey, one thing is for certain; you have to be an active participant. For most solutions, you are the one that has to go find them. They won't come to you.

What did I do to cope with all of this? I had to find therapy for all of these things that were coming at me from all angles. I found things that worked and things that didn't work.

Understanding The Extinction Burst

It is a familiar story; someone with a terminal illness slowly declines but, often, they have one short burst where they seem to be alert, well and recovering...and then they are gone.

This is something I refer to as an "Extinction Burst". I realize I'm not using the term within its proper clinical definition. In the clinical sense, when you are trying eliminate a bad habit, there seems to be this one last desperate attempt to revive it. For instance, when we change our diet to something healthy, we have a moment where we backslide and binge. Another instance would be when your computer dies and you keep hitting the power button over and over, trying to bring it back to life.

I think the term "Extinction Burst" can apply in a more abstract sense as well and not just in psychological circles. I think that, when a person is dying, an extinction burst happens when all the nerve endings cease to report back to the brain, and give the patient a false sense of recovery. If there are no signals of pain, then that means you are getting better, correct? It is an illusion and a warning that the patient is imminent to expire.

The Extinction Burst also happens when a person loses a limb and they experience the phenomenon known as "phantom pain" where they can still feel the amputated limb and are receiving pain signals from it. This is the body's final attempt to communicate with the absent limb. It is similar to that computer example I spoke of earlier; your body keeps pushing a dead on/off switch until it realizes the signal isn't returning.

Lastly, I think that, we who mourn are also experiencing an extinction burst. We have a brief time in the wake of a death where our energy is high because, similar to those non signals from dead nerve endings, we are ceasing to feel the proxy pain and suffering of a loved one. Their suffering has ended and, by association, so has our compassionate pain for them. This could be why many people experience a burst of energy shortly after a loved one passes. As many of us know, this is a short lived burst of energy before reality takes hold, and the pain and grieving begins.

If you experience a "high" after a loved one's death, it is not because you are dispassionate; it is because you are normal.

What Doesn't Work – Your Brain

It may seem facetious to say this but, the first thing that won't work in the wake of a loved one's passing is your brain. It is going to short circuit more than it usually does. The reason for this is that a death is an emotional injury. The side effects of an emotional injury are that you likely won't be thinking straight during this time. You will be forgetful and absent-minded. I want you to understand that this is normal. Do not get alarmed; it is a temporary condition and it will pass.

About two months after my dad's passing, I pulled my car up to a gas station pump and proceeded to do the routine task of filling my car with gas. It was a task I have performed hundreds of times with my current vehicle and it should have been second nature.

It wasn't.

My mind drew a blank as to where the tank cover release was. Without knowing where it was, I wouldn't be able to fill the car with gas. I sat there and thought, "What the hell? Where is it?" and had a moment of panic. There were dials everywhere in the car but no lever to release the tank cover. It was here somewhere! But where?

Fear and even more panic started to rise. I felt like I had lost my mind. Like a computer searching out a file and coming back with "file not found", my mind was unable to recall where a simple lever was that I had used hundreds of times with a car that I have owned for many years. Familiarity was now a stranger. My mind was drawing a vacuous and frightening blank.

After a few moments of sitting there in utter confusion, I opted to put the car in drive and admit defeat. I would maybe find the damned lever later. Or never! Maybe my car was just going to run out of gas and I'd have to park it forever because I was never going to be able to fill it again.

I looked down and, saw that the lever was to the left of the driver's seat by the car door. Just as it always was.

The recollection came back in a flood. "There you are!" I exclaimed. The relief that I had found the lever was almost overwhelming because it had been one of the scariest moments in my life; second only to watching my father in his death throes just a few months previous.

If you find that your brain doesn't work properly at this time, be assured that this is normal. Your brain is restarting after an emotional injury and just needs time to recalibrate itself. I know it is easier said than done, but be patient and your wits will return to you in time.

What Doesn't Work – Food, Addictions

What doesn't work? This one's easy. I turned to food. I would say to myself, "Screw it! My dad died. I'm going to eat this. I deserve it. I'm in pain!" And, I said it over and over again to the tune of almost 60 pounds later. Not only was I grieving, but I turned myself something that I was ashamed of and that I hated. And, there's no hiding an extra 60 pounds! It was out there for the entire world to see.

When people were brave enough to make a comment or ask about my weight gain, I would simply own up to it and tell them that I turned to food after my father died. I'd say I don't recommend doing that. The reaction I always got for that answer was a surprising amount of respect and compassion. I didn't run away from the answer; I faced, embraced and owned the answer. Denial and hiding would have done me no favours.

If you get one thing out of this presentation, make sure it's this: Don't medicate yourself with false safety blankets such as food. Those habits might have seemed like an escape hatch and an endorphin rush but, in actuality, it was a trap. They will be your undoing.

While I was the one who became a glutton and gained, my mother went the opposite and stopped eating. The weight that I gained was the weight that she lost. The bottom line is, don't make a major change in your eating habits. Be mindful and vigilant of this! This is one thing you cannot let slip.

I recommend a healthy diet plan. I guarantee it will change your life for the better. Limit your sugars, caffeine, gluten and starches. Yes, those things are hard to avoid as the siren call is very seductive! I can attest that a friend of mine followed a Paleo style of diet and was better able to control her anxiety and depression. I also found that, when I was eating healthy, I was able to better handle life's challenges.

I went away from the lifestyle because it was just easier to pull into a drive thru and have short term satisfaction. It turned into long term regret, shame and pain. I created a longer road to recovery because of it.

There are many lifestyle plans out there. The two that I recommend are the Paleo Diet and The Zone. Both of these are flexible and allow for cheat days. You are not married to either plan and can re-engage at any time. The only downside of them is, at the start, your body might go into sugar and caffeine withdrawal. You might feel worse at the start but, once your body releases the toxins and adjusts to the new you, you will feel better than you ever did.

What Doesn't Work – Isolation

When an animal gets wounded, they go away to maybe die or heal. It is a primal desire to go away and hide when a trauma is suffered. The reason behind it is simple; any other interaction requires precious resources that you could be using to help yourself heal faster. Cutting off the outside world frees those valuable resources so you can recover.

That's what I did; I withdrew and hid in my house. It was on rare occasions that I associated with friends or family. My mother was the only person who had regular access to my life at that time. Being around people only served to drain me of my energy which was in short supply during that time. I just didn't have it in my personal budget. I wanted to be left alone.

Then, through my own fault, it became a habit. I was unemployed at the time and many a day would find me not leaving my house. My day consisted of going from the bedroom, to the bathroom, to the couch, and to the kitchen; lather rinse and repeat. Any desire to make contact with the outside world became less and less important as my desire to just be left alone started to dominate my world. After awhile, that need to heal was being taken over by a depression brought on by isolation. As time went on, it was becoming clearer that I needed to bring balance to my life. I needed to explore the world and interact with people again.

Temporary isolation is necessary in order for you to gather your thoughts and recharge. It is also necessary to decompress once in awhile. Spending time alone at any time is a good thing. It is a good thing to get to know yourself.

Making it a habit, though, might not be in your best interests. You do need to find community eventually because we are social beings and need that connectivity with each other. As with most things suggested in this book, start slow and do what works best for you.

What Doesn't Work – Strenuous Exercise

I know this is going to sound counterintuitive but, believe it or not, exercise not only did *not* help me; it actually made things worse.

Why would this be?

In the wake of my dad's death, because I witnessed it, I was diagnosed with PTSD (Post Traumatic Stress Disorder). The high-end workouts that I had been doing at the gym were far too stressful on my body. Therefore, instead of reaping the benefits of exercise, I ended up putting my body under further distress. It contributed to my massive weight gain and made recovery from such workouts take far longer than normal.

I made the mistake of doing heavy workouts. What you should be doing is treating your grief like a physical injury. Consider yourself a rehab project and develop something that would befit someone with a major body injury.

This means you should be doing simple things like walking. This will at least keep the blood flowing in your body and it will likely mitigate the depth of grief you may have. Unless you are an elite athlete, start slow and work yourself back to normal again.

What Doesn't Work – Asking Why

Another thing that doesn't work is asking "Why"; Why did this happen? Why were they taken? Why, why, why? Never, ever ask this question!

Now, for some irony; why should you not ask why? Because, when you ask yourself a question, your brain is wired to find an answer. The worst open-ended question you can ask yourself is a "why" question. Your brain will go out there and find the first bit of information that fits and relay it back to you. It might be good information but, odds are, it's going to be bad and irrational.

For example:

Why were they taken from me?

Because, when you were a kid, you stole that pack of gum from the grocery store. Thought you were going to get away with it, now, didn't you? Or maybe it was that time you got in a fight with your loved one. And, now, you are paying for it because they are gone. It's ALL YOUR FAULT!

See what your mind does?

Instead of asking "why", ask the other questions; what, where, when, and how.

Where can I go to get some help?

When can I find the time to do this?

And the two most important questions you can ask:

How can I make good on this?

What can I learn from this?

Imagine the different answers you will get if you ask those questions instead of "why". Your brain is likely to come back with better, more productive answers.

What Doesn't Work – Being a Victim

What else doesn't work? Playing the victim card. I had PTSD, no job, my house was falling apart, my bank account was in free fall, and I gained a bunch of weight. My future prospects at the time were looking bleak. Would it have been fair to call me a victim?

I did this once...for about 30 seconds. I said to myself, I am a victim of what happened. The second I said that, I felt this awful helpless, *greasy* feeling fall over me. I had this suffocating feeling of powerlessness. It was awful and, 30 seconds later, I dumped that mentality and will never visit it again.

There is a victim in my story, and it's my dad. He has no recourse and no way back. So, by definition, he is a victim. I, on the other hand, am still standing. I still have the power to choose my direction.

You are only a victim if you want to be. I am standing before you today as NOT a victim but, as an advocate to tell you that you aren't alone and that there is a place on the other side of grief; it just takes time, effort, and patience on your part.

My horrible experience gave me two options; I can cower, wither and die inside or, I can step up and make good on this. The day after my dad's death, it was in me to make good on this. I owed it to myself and, most of all; I owed it to all of you.

Don't ever play the victim or it will prolong your grief indefinitely.

Prescription Drugs

The subject of the pharmaceutical industry conflicts me. It is like any tool; it does wonders when it is applied properly. However, when it is applied improperly, it can do well-intended harm. In the case of my dad, it was the "cure" that killed him.

My default position is that I am anti-drug because of my caution/mistrust of the system. I perceive an uncomfortable trend where doctors treat grief, anxiety and stress by giving you a once-over like you were livestock, writing on a notepad and saying, "Here, take this and, if it doesn't work, we'll try something else."

I understand that each of us experiences grief differently and these differences make the medical profession an inexact science at times. I understand that a doctor is only going by the information we give them and act accordingly. I understand that, unless our issue has an obvious solution, it becomes trial and error.

The issue I have is the perception of pill pushing as a solution instead of a bridge. In my opinion, pills are applied too quickly and hastily. It leaves me with this uncomfortable feeling that we, as patients, are mere product on an assembly line that are supposed to be shiny and new once we reach the end of the conveyor belt. It feels like there is an absence of humanity.

My opinion of pharmaceuticals is conflicted because, if a lot of us didn't go that route, will just find our own ways and do our own trial and error. Sometimes at our own peril.

As mentioned, my drug of choice was food. Did it help me deal with my grief? Briefly, yes. In the moment, yes. However, it was not a cure-all because I was still left with the issue at hand.

Once all the temporary relief was actualized, I was still left with the path of facing and dealing with my grief. The more I avoided it, the more I just stood on a road that stretched to the horizon. Medicating myself with food only made me stand still and delayed any forward progress. I came to the conclusion that this road wasn't going anywhere until I started walking on it. I had to face those things that were demanding to be addressed.

It wasn't until I faced my grief and saw it as a teaching tool that I started to feel the pain recede in drips and drops. I learned that, once you face those fears, you rob them of their power over you. I had to shift my perspective away from escapist self-indulgence to facing the root cause.

Medication is like a bandage meant to cover the wound to keep you from hemorrhaging. Most of the time, they are meant as a temporary solution until the real help comes to the rescue such as therapy or counseling. Medication is designed to give you the needed respite and recovery time so you have more strength to face the source of your hurt.

While my anti-drug stance is a personal choice, I do not begrudge its application. I am a staunch believer that our road to recovery is unique and personal. What works for one may or may not work for another. There is no shame in seeking this kind of help. But do so with your eyes open in the knowledge that, most of the time, it is a bridge.

Counseling

Speaking of what works for one may not work for another, professional counseling didn't work for me. It is not that the counselors were unqualified or incompetent; it was that it was not what I needed.

Perhaps my expectations of finding a silver bullet in counseling was the issue. Perhaps it was the fact that it felt like a one-way conversation and the exercises I was given often felt gimmicky. The whole experience of counseling, for me, was like fitting a square peg into a round hole. Neither of us was wrong; we just weren't a fit and we had to part ways.

With that said, I have a great admiration for counselors and strongly recommend going to one. They are a pair of objective, professional eyes that can view your situation from a distance without emotional involvement. They can offer you solutions and can help you see things in a different light.

Please do not be discouraged if you tried counseling and it didn't work for you. It just means that you required something else.

What Doesn't Work – Avoiding Your Grief

You can delay grief all you like – years & decades even! – but all it will do is wait. You can deny and play like it isn't affecting you. You can run away in your mind and do all the distractions you please. But you will find that grief is patient and, when ignored, it is unkind.

Grief, when ignored, won't get smaller and it won't dissipate. It will just sit on a lofty perch, watch you, and wait. And when the time is most opportune, when you are finally open to facing it, it will be there...and it will be like the death happened yesterday.

Time does not heal. Time only puts distance between you and the event. If you are trying to avoid your grief and "running out the clock" like it has an expiry date, you will discover that your heart does not know the meaning of the concept of time.

What works – Talking About It

Just like you cannot isolate yourself for a long time, you cannot be silent about your loss for a long time. You *need* to talk about the one you lost. There is no way around it.

While this does tie in to the section on counselling, you do need to talk about your loved one with friends and family as well. The reason is because those friends and family can relive those cherished memories with you. It will allow you to share healing laughter and tears. This is the support system that will get you through the initial shock.

There are downsides to talking about it, however. There are people around you who may get annoyed at this form of therapy. This is where you might hear the infamous phrase, "Get over it". If you hear that, do not take it personally because, as already addressed earlier in this book, it's not about you; it's about them. Those people just cannot relate or understand, and that's okay. Leave those people be. Perhaps, one day, when a major loss visits them, you can reach out and lend an ear to them. Don't be resentful. Don't keep score.

There is one caution to talking about it; avoid complaining as much as you can. Complaining does nothing to honour the one who has passed and does nothing to honour you. It is similar to declaring yourself a victim. Complaining is also repelling to the people around you and it is something that becomes tedious to listen to after awhile. A little bit of complaining is understandable and expected; chronic complaining without seeking resolution is tiresome for both you and your circle of friends.

Therein lies the key to complaining; it is pointless without attempting to find a resolution.

Rebellion

In the midst of all the chaos, I felt powerless with all the forces that were coming against me. I had often blamed my dad for many of them because, well, *he cancelled the insurance!* Had he not done that, his estate would have been rather easy to clean up. Instead, it was like a post-apocalyptic wasteland filled with snipers targeting me every day.

Short of bringing my dad back to life so I could admonish him for all that happened and have him apologize, I hadn't a method of recourse to take any control of anything in my life. That is, until I invented one.

Remember the Claddagh Ring? I wore it proudly after my dad had given it to me. My dad was actually honoured to the point of tears when I had gotten it resized the very next day. He was proud that I wanted to wear it as soon as possible. I told him I look forward to the day when I could wear it in the "married" position. It was something that held a deep meaning for both of us.

As a measure of protest, I decided to not wear the Claddagh ring until the estate was finalized. This was my rebellion; my way of kicking ass and taking names. Outside of my home, it was a pointless gesture as people hardly noticed whether I was wearing the ring or not. In my mind, though, it was a defiant, repudiating gesture. One that would teach my dad a lesson.

We all know that I didn't teach anyone a lesson by doing this, but in some way, it allowed me to have control over *one thing* in my life. Just one thing! If making the ghost of my dad stand there and watch while I took off the ring he gave me, and put it in a box in my dresser until such time that I could wear it again, then so be it; this is how he was going to "learn" to never do that again. Take that!

As empty a gesture as it was, it allowed me to have something within my purview. It gave me a small piece of earth upon which I could stand and call my own. I could begin to build my world again from this tiny, empty gesture. I want you to understand that this wasn't a gesture of hate; it was a gesture of rebellion and self-preservation.

It took many months, but the day came when I opened the dresser drawer, took out the box, and placed the ring on my finger again. It was a personal gesture of forgiveness and brought a symbolic end to a dark and desperate time.

What Works – Understanding the Purpose of Suffering

Ask yourself: When things are perfect and you have a utopia around you, do you learn anything?

The answer is probably no.

From my experience, the greatest learning comes from times of crisis. The greatest learning comes from when you are put to the test. When things are perfect, you are not being rested, not tested.

I liken it to a former body builder who said, "How do I get these muscles? I don't get them by sitting around. I don't get them by being in a state of bliss. I get them by putting the greatest amount of pressure – the greatest amount of force – against these muscles. And, how do those muscles respond? They get bigger! They get stronger! Because they get bigger and stronger, I am better equipped to handle opposition."

When I searched for meaning in my own suffering, I think that the ultimate outcome was I become a stronger person. Had I not become that, then the loss of my father would have been for naught. I chose to be thankful for the opportunity to learn in spite of a tribulation. I used a crisis to learn about myself and the world. And to maybe help you.

That is how I view the purpose in all of this. I encourage you to find the purpose in yours.

What Works – Humour

One of the things that worked was a sense of humour. I happened to develop a very dark sense of humour; a humour that sometimes made other people uncomfortable. You might need to surround yourself with people who "get" and understand this because, you are going to get a lot of shocked looks if you unleash one of these dark punch lines in the company of people who don't understand and are easily offended.

I guess I learned that from my dad because he used humour to deal with his condition. My dad was borderline diabetic and, after his cancer diagnosis, his diabetes *magically* disappeared. It was one of those odd things.

So, my dad said, "Hey! I found a cure for diabetes! It's cancer."

After my father's death, there was one time when I was visiting my mom. During the visit, she went downstairs and became quiet. I understood that, when my mom becomes quiet like that, it is time to seek her out because something is going on.

I would discover that my mom was going through dad's things and packing them up. Dad had made a pact with mom that, when one of them die, the other would immediately pack up the other's stuff and give it away. They both knew that this was a way of being able to move on with their lives.

As I saw my mom was in tears, I decided to help. I would go through dad's belongings and come across a cigar I had given him from a trip I took to the Dominican Republic. It had been in his desk drawer for years and was dry and unusable.

I said to mom, "What the hell? He never smoked the cigar I gave him!" I then paused and said, "Oh right; smoking gives you cancer."

Mom raised her head, guffawed and stopped. She wagged a finger at me and said, "Darcy…that's funny. But, too soon."

I smiled and said, "I tried."

Mom smiled back and said, "You did. It will be funny one day."

I could see that my mom appreciated the effort, but she wasn't quite there yet to make fun of a bad situation. To her credit, she didn't take offense and understood what I was attempting to do. The joke would be funny another day when things weren't so fresh.

Poking fun at the situation and finding humour in it will also lessen the power grief has over you. Humour in these situations is not cold and unfeeling; it is life affirming and defiant because you choose how you are going to react. Instead of being at the mercy of sadness, you are taking back some of the control you may have lost. Laughing through tears is a sign of strength and perseverance.

As with anything, though, humour must also be used in moderation. If it is your only means of healing, then humour can quickly turn into avoidance and denial of grief.

What Works – Prayer & Meditation

As I have already established, I would not say that I am a religious person. That being said, I would be remiss if I did not include the real benefits of processing grief through prayer and meditation. Both of these are important tools to calming the internal chaos.

My favourite way to describe the difference between prayer and meditation is that prayer is for talking to God while meditation is for listening to God. I like how each, while similar, are very different in application.

I believe we are spiritual beings and prayer and meditation should be an important part of our grieving process. Scientific studies have shown that positive changes occur in brain chemistry during prayer or meditation. Whatever your belief system, they offer an opportunity for reflection and a way to come to terms with your loss.

Prayer and meditation aren't necessarily the exclusive domain of religion. It can be argued that the sections that follow – Journaling, Music, Drawing, and Little Notes – apply the same principles as meditation and prayer. Journaling is the active and silent meditation where you process your thoughts onto paper (or screen as it were). Little Notes is similar to prayer in that you are privately speaking into the air about your loved one.

Other things you can do that are similar to prayer or meditation are to go out in the country and listen to nature. You can also go on a scenic drive or go to a park and people watch. Anything that allows you to clear your thoughts and quiet the mind are forms of meditation.

What Works – Music

This one was so obvious I almost left it out of the book. Music is a common language among us and has the power to move us in all the range of emotions available. It has the power to move us through and beyond time.

The way I employed music was to create a soundtrack. I am a fan of movie scores and have dozens of them (yes, some friends mock me for my unusual taste in music). I took all this beautiful music and created a movie score to my situation. I listened for the happy notes of when my dad was still alive and the relationship we had built. Then, it was time for the crisis and, eventual passing. I ended the soundtrack with notes that spoke of hope and remembrance.

I had often said that it is better to watch a movie than to live a movie. For one terrible day, I lived a movie and, through music, I put a soundtrack to it. Movies often have a resolution where a main character either has a happy ending or finds a way to move forward in life. Having a soundtrack to my grief allowed me to see beyond the pain of today and look forward to a time when the chapter would draw to a close and the credits would roll.

What Works – Sketching/Drawing

Drawing or sketching is a in the same vein as meditation in that your mind is focused on the task at hand. Creating something feels good as it is life affirming and gives us purpose.

You don't have to be a professional artist to draw. If you can express your drawing to show the emotions you have during this time, you will find that those feelings flow out of you through your pen or pencil; even if it is just an angry scribble. Your intent is not to put together an exhibit and sell your artwork; the intent is to give the negative emotions a place to express themselves and find an exit door.

What Works – Journaling

So, what works in the long term? Journaling is the number one thing that worked for me. It was just something that I started on my own. I had heard many times that this is a very therapeutic thing to do.

I want you to understand that this is a process. It isn't going to be a silver bullet that takes away all the pain at once. It is not a drive-thru solution.

In case you are wondering, there is *NO* drive-thru solution.

Once you have accumulated numerous entries, you will start to feel better. Some of your journal entries will be short. Some will be these long diatribes. Some of the entries will be beautiful works of literature. Some of them will be absolutely terrible. Many of them will just be random. But, the most important thing that I want you to remember is:

THIS NOT FOR ANYONE ELSE! THIS IS FOR YOU!

You don't need to be a literary giant to start a journal. You are not going to sell it to a publisher. Who cares what your writing talents are! Nobody is going to see it. Let the emotions leave through your fingertips.

I do promise you that, once you have a journal for over a year – and, it's going to take a year! – You can look back on it to see how far you have progressed. This is why journaling can be a valuable measuring stick.

Another thing you will notice from reading your journal is that you will be able to recognize certain patterns within yourself. It is inevitable to see a repetitive theme in your journal entries that will shine a light on a constructive or destructive habit. This will give you a chance to do some introspection and maybe change a bad habit to something more beneficial. For example, one thing I noticed about myself was that, for a period of time, all I did was play the same video game for hours on end. My journal revealed how much time I was wasting on this form of escapism. I didn't like that many of my journal entries ended with "played video game for the rest of the day". It unveiled a bad habit and gave me the opportunity to remedy a part of my life that was not beneficial.

What Works – Little Notes

Another thing that works? This is my mom's idea; write personal notes to the deceased.

My dad's ashes were spread at one of his favourite hideaways to observe wildlife. Remember when I talked about anchors? This is an important psychological anchor for me to go and gather my thoughts.

Wherever your loved one resides, be it where you spread the ashes or where the grave site is, go and visit the site once in awhile. And take a note with you, hand-written if possible. Think of it as a one-way conversation between you and the deceased. Go to the place, leave the note, and say a few words to the air. For such a simple gesture, it is very therapeutic and helps you organize your thoughts to process your grief.

Don't believe me? Just try it once and I can bet you will leave with a sense of peace. No one needs to know.

A Cautionary Tale

Before I conclude this section, I have a cautionary tale for you:

If you wallow in bitterness and anger, sometimes, the world is going to hit back and, the lesson you learn will not be gentle. When these things happen, consider it "corrective action" or "discipline".

Months after my dad's passing, I went to the hospital to retrieve his records. It was a hard thing to do because the hospital is an extreme trigger for me. If you take 100 steps inside the front doors and turn to the left, you can see the hallway where it all occurred. It is right there as a painful reminder. There is no avoiding it.

I walked in the front doors and had an immediate "fight or flight" response as if I was in enemy territory. Every single staff member I saw I viewed as an enemy. I had a primal and visceral reaction to them.

I saw a doctor walking with a muffin in his hand and I thought, *"...and how many did you kill?"*

I looked over and saw a nurse in line for coffee and thought again, *"...and how many did you kill?"*

I did this over and over; nurses, doctors, even admin staff and janitors! It was the prevailing, hair-trigger thought; *"...and how many did you kill?"*

It was then that I saw a nurse walking up the hallway and, as this accusation was becoming far too easy for me, I started again, *"...and how many did –"*

I stopped. That nurse was familiar. That nurse was my friend. I knew her heart and I knew her ethics. I had the sudden and cathartic realization that what I was doing was vitriolic and unfair. It stabbed me in the heart that I was accusing, of all people, a trusted friend in this manner.

It would be weeks later when I was hanging out with this same friend. I would confess to her this experience, the bitterness I had, and how I was about to say in my head to her, "...and how many did you kill?"

Her response? She leaned in, looked me in the eyes and said with the utmost sincerity, "I am sorry."

She wasn't apologizing for herself. That sorry was not just for what had happened to me; it was also on behalf of her colleagues who failed me that day.

It was the first time that I had received any kind of apology from medical staff after what I had witnessed. There was a little bit of healing there. There was a little bit of reconciliation there.

I know that doctor didn't wake up on that fateful day and say, "I'm purposely going to make a mistake and take a life today." I just wanted to hear that someone was sorry.

Well, I got my sorry. But, not before I created self-inflicted pain.

In case you are wondering, that was the only time, in all the years I have known this friend, that I saw her walking the hallways at work. Coincidence?

This is a great segue to my last piece of advice:

Strange Things Will Happen

It is time to talk about the elephant in the room; the thing that most people avoid because they may feel silly. Well, I'm going to be silly and talk about the elephant in the room.

My last piece of advice is: Embrace the strange things that may happen after a loved one's passing. Coincidence or not; embrace them!

Strange things started happening during my dad's death throes and, many strange things happened after his passing. I'll share just two of *many* stories I have of the strange and wonderful.

Strange Things – The Dream

I spent a year unemployed to wrangle the estate and deal with my veritable cocktail of negative emotions – shaken and stirred. I eventually ran out of time to make mortgage payments on my house and, I had to leave. I was offered a job in Calgary so, I sold my house in Regina and made plans to move there. I had planned on starting a whole new life and leaving this bloody nightmare behind.

The day I sold my house, my dad appeared to me in a dream. He said, "You can't take that job." and I asked why. He said, "I can't tell you. But something is coming for you, and it's soon."

I was like, "Gee, dad, it's a little late because *I SOLD THE HOUSE* and I'm moving...partly *BECAUSE OF YOU!*" And I proceeded to get into a fight with him. I said, "Either you tell me or I'm just going to go!"

Dad sits back and says, "I can't tell you. But it's coming for you...and it's soon."

I reply, "If you can't tell me, then I have to go. Sorry!"

Basically, it was me saying, screw you, dad. The dream would end with my father getting upset with me.

So, I move to Calgary, buy a new condo and I proceeded to start a new life. Well, wouldn't you know it, 7 weeks later; I get a phone call from the University of Regina. They offered me a dream job that I have to this day. When I hung up the phone, I didn't rejoice at the wonderful career opportunity. I simply said, "Dammit, dad was right..."

What was I going to do? Tell my boss in Calgary that I couldn't work for him because I had a bad dream? I didn't take the leap of faith I was asked to take.

...or, was it all just a coincidence? And, am I crazy?

So, for a year, I offered the condo in Calgary to my mom to stay there and look after it while, I looked after her apartment in Moose Jaw. And, if you're keeping score; I lived in Moose Jaw, worked 60 kilometers away in Regina, and owned property 700 kilometers away in Calgary.

All because I didn't pay heed to a possible coincidence...or was it?

As a side note, the house I sold in Regina? It flooded 2 months after I sold it. First time that ever happened in that neighborhood. Had I still been living in that house, it is something that would have wiped me out financially.

"...I'm Okay..."

Probably the most visceral strange encounter happened in the first hour of my father's passing. This is a story where you can accept, reject, or dismiss it by explaining it away.

Let's go back to January 30th, 2010. It's about 45 minutes after my dad has passed. I'm in my own world as I walk out of the hospital. My mind is pretty much blank and numb after what had just happened. I am walking out of the hospital and, once I step into the sunlight, I feel this thing that feels like...an annoyance. Like a fly that buzzes by your temple...but it's January! At first, I am annoyed at this and it feels like I need to wave it away.

...I'm okay...

And, then, I felt it move around me, my right to left and then what felt like a hand on my forehead...

...I'm okay...I'm okay...I'm okay...

In the studies that have been done regarding Near Death or Shared Death Experiences, many people who claim to have had them, say they are in the presence of something that is so powerful and so loving that, you would give up everything – *EVERYTHING!* – in your life to go with it.

Well, that's what this felt like; the illusion of this world stood down in favour of what I felt was the purest of pure love. It would be the most beautiful, most poetic, most perfect moment of my entire life.

And, as gentle as it came to me, stayed a few moments, and went away on the light breeze of that chilly afternoon, it left me behind in a bittersweet moment that hasn't come close to being duplicated before or since.

Can you explain it away with the imaginations of a grieved mind desperately looking for a way to cope? Or is it something else? That one is for you to decide.

Despite the way my father died, despite the aftermath, the anger the bitterness, all that. To me, the ultimate message in this is an all-encompassing, all-hopeful, all-loving message spoken softly:

"I'm okay".

Through death, through grief, and, eventually, healing; if "I'm okay", then so too shall you be.

Thank you for your time.

☙

Questions

The first time I gave this presentation, the Q&A had some of the most thought provoking questions I could imagine. I was amazed at the depth of what people asked.

Do you still experience "the strange things"?

Yes. In fact, there are some stories in the following section of this book that attest to this. One story I did not put in this book was that, in the days after my father's passing, the phone would ring and go straight to the messages on the answering machine. Mom had an old style answering machine at the time. When the answering machine would pick up, it would go through messages, selecting only bill collectors and passing over everyone else. It did this several times over the course of a week even when the order of the messages had changed; it would still skip over regular messages and play the bill collectors. The last time it occurred, my sister blurted out, "Dad, you are scaring me! Stop it!" The scanning of the messages immediately stopped when she said that and, after that day, it never happened again.

I have also had several dreams about my father after his passing. Some are innocuous while others were more profound. I do remember one where he gave me a brief hug and thanked me for "Looking after Mither." *Mither* was one of dad's catch phrases he used instead of "Mother". That was how he referred to his wife – my mother – in front of his children.

One of the reasons why I do not believe these events are self-delusion is that they are a string of coincidences. One event can easily be considered coincidence and be dismissed. Many of them strung together, however, brought me to question if it was something *other* than coincidence.

You mentioned that your siblings didn't help. Did you ask them for help?

No, I did not. That is a great question because I realized that I projected my own standards onto them. I made the assumption that, it's your parents, do you really need to be asked? Isn't it just a natural thing to come to your parent's aid when they need you?

It appears that while I made assumptions about them, they made assumptions about me. Or, they made assumptions that *someone* would take care of things so they didn't have to.

I guess, if I didn't ask them for help, I am partly culpable for the fact that they didn't help.

You are right; I should have asked.

You had two important questions you should ask yourself; "How can I make good on this" and "What can I learn from this". So, how would you answer those questions?
Wow, that's a fantastic question! I guess if I'm going to walk the talk, I best answer these!

How do I make good on this? By doing what I'm doing now. I have a voice and I'm a confident writer. I'm giving you a venue to know you aren't alone. Death is a common experience for all of us and a lot of us have a tough time talking about it. Well, I'm here to talk about it.

What did I learn from this? Wow...well, I learned that my belief in God certainly isn't wasted. It reinforced it. I learned a lot of good things because of that.

On the flip side, I learned that you can't completely trust people in the hospital and the system in general. I also learned that some people will try to take advantage of you when you are most vulnerable; sadly, I count some family among them. I also got to experience the ruthless side of bill collectors. That's the unfortunate side. I learned a lot of good and a lot of bad.

Probably the most valuable things that I learned were about myself. It made me aware of my strengths and weaknesses. To know one's self is probably the hardest thing to do in this life.

Was the procedure done on your dad related to his cancer?

No it was not. And, this is something you need to be vigilant about when it comes to the system. My dad was considered palliative which means they should *not* have done anything invasive to him. Instead, they manipulated my dad, tinkered around and, you know the result.

One thing I encourage everyone to be is a vigilant advocate for your loved one. Doctors, nurses and other support staff are *not* your advocates. They are there to help, yes, but they are not obligated to be your advocate. That is *your* job!

Another one of the disturbing trends I have witnessed in health care is the performance of superfluous, invasive procedures on palliative patients. What is the motivation for this? Is it money? Are they using the patients for practice? Does it further medical science in any way?

Things I have learned from this experience is that some doctors will attempt to divide you from the vulnerable patient and convince them that they need this extra procedure even though they are considered palliative. The doctor will cite their authority in the medical field in a deified manner as though patients should bow down and worship them. I have witnessed the use of manipulation to scare the palliative patient into accepting the invasive procedure. Part of the manipulation is dismissing or mocking family members who question it.

When a palliative patient is on mind altering drugs like morphine, it is the job of the advocate – usually a spouse or close family member – to be the decision maker on behalf of the patient. At the very least, the advocate needs to be consulted. What I have witnessed has been an end-around maneuver to bypass that.

I realize that my experience might be unique. But I have my suspicions that it is regular practice.

The bottom line is, you know you are doing a good job when the doctor is not impressed with you. It is not your job to be their friend, a "yes" person or to "go along to get along". Question everything and always be reminded that doctors are human, and when they make mistakes, it is often fatal.

Is your mom upset with your siblings as much as you are?

In a word; *YES!* I think, in some ways, even moreso. It struck her in the heart as a parent and made her turn the issue on herself and question whether she was a good mom or not. It made my dad question whether he was a good dad or not. If you ever want to hurt your mom or dad, not only tell them they are a bad parent, but *show* them by not being there when they need you the most.

One of the events that broke it for me was about a year after my dad was diagnosed. Two of my sisters had pretty much abandoned my dad; they'd never visit, phone, and rarely email. And when they were in contact, they had attempted to divide my parents by playing one against the other. They only served to cause strife and conflict when my parents needed support. It was then that I messaged them and told them both "If this is all you can offer as far as 'support', then please be a stranger."

That would be the one time they would actually listen to me. Not because I was right; but because it was an easy way out and a wonderful excuse to paint me as the villain again. I was fine with shouldering the blame for their absence from that point onward. It was better that I be the lightning rod rather than my parents. I was strong at the time and could stand in the line of fire.

I still remember the night my dad and I were spending time together in his living room. He fought back tears when the subject of those two came up. He said, "What did I ever do to them?" and he broke down.

As you know, my dad was not one to show emotions like that. But, to be broken down like that was a step too far for me. I was *beyond* angry.

What had my father done to them? Let me tell you what he did to them: he brought home a regular paycheque the entire time they lived at home; they never went hungry because of him even though finances were tough many times; he encouraged them their entire lives to be educated because that was how you make it in this world; he walked them down the aisle for each of their weddings; he did everything a *good* and *decent* father would do.

Now that I am older and see all that my dad did for me, I am reminded of a line from a song; "My life has been a poor attempt to imitate the man."

That was what was sitting before me in tears, questioning whether he was a good father or not.

He would go to his final breaths wondering what he had done to deserve the treatment he received. My wayward sisters would come to my dad's deathbed…and proceed to discuss the deal on shoes they had gotten at Walmart. I wonder to this day if that puerile, inane discussion was born out of guilt for not being there for their father. I often wonder if it was a deflection to save face.

My parent's issue with my siblings is a deeper hurt when you compare it to my anger. I didn't raise the people who are my brother and sisters. I don't have the vested interest that my parents did.

And while I have written off my siblings, my parents would have taken them back with open arms and attempted to rebuild what was lost. Such is the unconditional love of a *good* parent. These are the things my siblings never took the time to see; for reasons I cannot fathom, my parent's love for them was unconditional.

Is my mom upset with my siblings? In a word; yes.

How should you be a friend to someone who lost someone?

It's real simple; listen to them. Give them space when they need it. But, check in on them if you've not heard from them in awhile. Sometimes, we need isolation. Isolation is not a bad thing. But, there can be too much of it.

You might hear them talk about their loved one for a long time after, and yes, sometimes it can be trying because the stories can be repetitive. But just be a friend and listen. They don't want you to "fix" them. They just want to be heard when they unload. Nothing more than that.

You said you went to get your dad's records. How did you do that? My husband passed away 6 months ago and they never told me the cause of death. I want his records.

Remember when I said that I *felt* like I was in enemy territory in the hospital after returning there? Well, you *ARE* in enemy territory when you go to the records department! Their job is to stall you and do everything they can to prevent you from getting the records. Be it through intimidation or stonewalling you, their unofficial job is to make it difficult for you even though you have every right to see those records.

Now, since your husband died 6 months ago, it will be tougher because that is still within the statute of limitations. They will freely release his records after two years have passed because they are no longer legally culpable. Any time before two years, they consider you a threat even if you are inquiring just for the sake of closure. Be very aware of that.

Because you are the spouse, you have first rights to the records. No one else can gain access to them behind your back. As is the law here in Saskatchewan, the spouse has the first rights to the records until that spouse dies. When the spouse is gone, the children are next in line to have first right of refusal to see the records. And, it goes on down from there.

So do not worry if you feel someone in your family can go behind your back because they can't. They need written permission from you.

Do you get all the records? You have to be careful what you specify as they can always conveniently leave something out because you didn't ask for it. You have to make sure your request says that you require *all* of the records.

Again, do you get all of the records? How do you know if anything was taken out? That, I don't know. I guess, in this case, you just have to trust.

There is a fee for the records – usually a cost per page – and that is something you have to ask up front. Be prepared to spend in upwards of 300 dollars just for the privilege of seeing property that legally belongs to you.

One last comment from an audience member:

Another women talked about how she could relate to the issue of family strife. She referred to herself as being a "recovering hater" and said she has the same issues with her siblings. She said, they don't deserve forgiveness but they do deserve mercy.

You need to give mercy when you can't forgive.

I thought it was a beautiful comment. And, I am stealing the term "recovering hater".

☙

AFTER THE MOURNING AFTER:
Other Stories of Death, Grief and Healing

My Dad's Eulogy

"I'm here! I'm here! Oh Glory Be!"

This is what I'm sure my dad said when he first arrived in heaven. Dad was one to pull out such...unique phrases. For instance, it wasn't "chit chat" it was "Chitty Chatty". It wasn't a "Minute"; it was a "Minootie". It wasn't "Credit Union", it was a "Credit Onion".

Ah ha ha...ya dad, that's funny. And, then we'd roll our eyes.

Dad was also the only person I've ever known who could watch endless hours of The Weather Network. It's like, okay, dad, it said the same temperature about 2 hours ago. Can we change the channel now? Yes, yes, I know! The conditions could change. But, you know what? We're inside!

But dad was unapologetic for it. It's who he was and, well, that was Jimmy Boy. A man of his own making.

Dad was born to proud parents, Margaret and Francis, in 1936. According to Francis, dad was a stubborn child as exhibited by his abject refusal to get his hair cut when he was sent to the barber. Dad would fight and struggle and it would take 2 and 3 people just to hold him down before the job was able to get done. And, why would dad want his fiery Irish red locks cut anyway? I mean, come on! Who doesn't like red hair, right?

Dad's love of nature was cultivated early on in his life as he spent much of his childhood outdoors, having adventures in the meadows and the fields of Ancaster, Ontario. Dad also discovered one of the first major passions in his life; flying. He had enrolled in the airborne militia and, despite having perfect 20/20 vision, was rejected because of a rare oddity; you see, one of his eyes was far sighted and one of his eyes was near sighted. They perfectly balanced out to a 20/20 vision. But, unfortunately, this was not acceptable and, life had to turn in a new direction. Being a military pilot was not meant to be.

Dad eventually went to University in Guelph. Life in southern Ontario was starting to become too congested for him and he was called to move to the open spaces out west. Dad ended up trying his hand at a match making company called "Lonely Hearts Club". It was similar to what online dating is today. And, through the letters he sent, he ended up meeting a woman from Broadview, Saskatchewan who would eventually become his wife of 46 years, Rose.

Now, things didn't get off to that romantic start that you might have thought with such storybook romances. No, not at all. Remember when I said, who doesn't like red hair? Well, apparently, my mom – Rose – didn't! He had sent her a picture and she was so disappointed in his red hair that she stopped writing him. To dad's credit, he kept up the pursuit of Rose and, to make a long story short, they would be married in 1963.

After one child and a massive house fire later, the new family moved out west to Saskatchewan where dad had wanted to be all along. They would eventually have 5 children in all and, to date, they have 10 grandchildren.

Dad's career would be one of a civil servitude. After small stints as a teacher and a Wheat Pool employee, Dad would eventually become an agrologist with what is now Saskatchewan Agriculture and Food. This was the perfect job for dad in that it melded his love of science as well as his love of the outdoors. Dad also loved to help people and this was a great way to help out in Saskatchewan's biggest industry.

Dad would be an Agrologist for 35 years, not missing a single day due to illness. Dad was the epitome of a strong work ethic. He was a man of honour, integrity, and loyalty. Not just to his job but to his family as well. He is a great example for all of us to follow.

Among the many of dad's hobbies, he was one of the most knowledgeable war history buffs I've ever known. Dad could recite, almost verbatim, all the battles of the Second World War. He knew all the politics, all the generals, all the pass codes. Dad knew it all, backwards and forwards. Anytime Dad was near an air museum, he had to proudly tell you the make, model, and history of each plane in there. He could even tell you some of the planes he had actually flown in. One of his favourites is the Lancaster plane in the The Nanton Lancaster Society Air Museum in Ancaster, Ontario.

Dad was a mover and a shaker. Well...how about just a mover. Let's see if I can name all the places Dad, Mom and Family lived in. Are you ready? Here we go: Regina, Whitewood, Broadview, North Battleford, Kelvington, Shaunavon, Yorkton, Coronach, and, lastly for Dad, Moose Jaw. It's a good thing that my parents are super social people because all that moving might have had a terrible impact on their psyche. Dad and Mom made friends easily and, even on Dad's last day on this earth, he was a vehicle to allow me to get the email address of a new friend we met in the waiting room. Dad was a chitty chatty type of guy.

I'm sure that, if you look around the church today, you will see a diverse group of individuals from all corners of the province. Look around, there are old and new friends here. My parents have touched a great many lives and have made a great many friends. So, after the service, go forth and share your stories about Dad. It's his day today!

They say "Ashes to ashes, Dust to dust". It is those times between the dusts when it is our opportunity to make an impact on the world; to leave it in a better place that which we started.

Take some time today to think about what Jim did for you. Did he make you smile? Did he make you laugh? Take the time today to remember that piece of you that was forever changed by him.

Let me share an example. The most memorable vacation of my life was spent with my parents in October of 2008. They had sat me down one day and asked if I would tour them around Mount Rushmore in South Dakota. They had never been that far down into The United States, ever, and I jumped at the opportunity to show them around. It was, in a word, magical. I never would have thought that I could get along with my parents in one hotel room and in a small car for 9 days straight. We were in close quarters and I thought this was going to be a challenge. But, I had an AMAZING time with them.

We stayed in the small town of Keystone and dad was in love with this leather shop across the street from the hotel. It was this amazing leather shop that sold high quality leather jackets for 100 bucks. And, the place was owned by a Vietnam vet. Dad was in heaven! Inexpensive high quality leather products and a War Veteran to share stories with. What could be better? I mean, there were 2 or 3 mornings in those 9 days where I woke up alone in the hotel room, wondering where my parents were. And, just a simple walk across the street to the leather shop would be my answer. The owner of the leather shop loved my mom and dad and, since it was the slow season, encouraged them to come in every day just to "chitty chatty".

It was the best of times that would, sadly, turn into the most challenging of times. During the trip, I had been suspicious of dad's ability to eat and swallow. I had suspected something was wrong. And, as I drove them all over the Badlands of South Dakota, I had this bad feeling that this was a last hurrah for dad.

And, it was.

Even as I watched dad physically reduce before my eyes over the next 15 months, I discovered this man of inner strength and determination. Dad outlived not one, not two, but four death sentences. He far outlived most predictions and this is a testament to his healthy living and fortitude. He showed me that he had the Lion Heart of the soldier he always wanted to be.

For some insight into who my dad is, please allow me to share the last words I had with him alone as he lay on the bed, unresponsive, awaiting his appointment with The Lord:

"Dad? I came to say farewell for now. But, just for now. I want to say thank you for everything. Especially these past 15 months. I've been wondering what purpose it served to have a man be perfectly healthy for the first 72 years of his life, only to have a disease take him in his 73rd. Well, dad, although the purpose is different for everyone, I think I found the purpose in all of this for me.

"I got to see a side of you I never saw before. You know how a child first sees his dad as infallible? And, then, in their teen years, all that admiration is washed away and the parent now does *nothing* right and the child wonders how in the world they could be related to them. And then later on, it comes to a balance.

"Well, dad, these past 15 months went deeper than just that. I got to see you not only through the eyes of a son. I got to see you through the eyes of your siblings. I got to see you through the eyes of your childhood friends. I saw you with the same vulnerabilities in your youth as I did. But, I also saw you with the same youthful dreams and aspirations...like I did. You showed me that you won some and you showed me that you lost some. You let me see the moments of heartbreak in your life. But, you also showed me more than enough that your heart can be fulfilled. And, you have with your wife and my mom, Rose. I mean, your heart was so full of love for her that it was like a balloon about to burst.

"And, all those times when you had your chemo treatments. And, you looked up at me with those bright blue eyes and smiled when I arrived; you emanated an unconditional love that only a parent could give. I could feel that!

"You let me see all of this in yourself in the past year.

"Most of all, dad, you let me see that you were, indeed, human. And, you have given me the permission to be human myself; a perfectly, imperfect human being who is forever changed by you and these last 15 months. I will never be the same again because of the time I got to spend with you in the past year and a bit. You have facilitated the birth of a whole new person and I am happy with what you created in me.

"While it's hard to let you go, I would not trade the experience of walking with you on this final journey. We were shoulder to shoulder and we fought this one hard. You are, and ever shall be, my Winston Churchill who *never* surrendered. Even into your last and finest hour.

"We'll meet again. And, when we do, tell you what; if there is a Credit Onion in heaven, we can meet there first and we can Chitty Chatty for a minootie again like we used to. And, this one time only, I'll let YOU buy lunch! You don't have to worry about me stealing the bill and paying behind your back. Okay? God Bless you, Dad.

"We love you."

☙

When Does It Stop Hurting So Much?

There are times when you don't need to be in regular contact with a friend to see that someone in their family is reaching the end of their life. There is an air of "grief prep" when these things happen.

I watched online as a friend of mine kept posting pictures of her mother with regularity. I found this odd as she was one to post pictures of her trips and the odd social gathering; rarely would she post family. She wasn't a frequent poster to begin with but, to see her mother becoming a regular theme for a period of time started to make me question whether she was in a pre-grief mode as a loved one declines.

Weeks later, I would get my answer as I would see several postings from friends, offering condolences on the loss of her mother. I joined in these condolences and noted that this was the fourth year in a row where one of my circle (including myself) would lose a parent. I was the second one of my group to go through this and, I was getting well versed in what to expect when you lose someone close to you.

I simply offered to lend an ear should she need it. I told her I had "been there, done that, and now give tours". I said so thinking that she would be surrounded by family and other friends and, that I'd never hear from her. If she should come forward to me, my offer of an ear would be valid and not some empty platitude.

A few short weeks would pass when I would see an email from her. It was one simple sentence:

When does it stop hurting so much???

Such a valid question! I knew that I couldn't spin the pain one feels with the loss of a parent into something that would "kiss and make it all better". That would be a disservice to my friend who asked an honest question. It is a question that all of us ask in the middle of grief.

So, having "been there, done that" complete with t-shirt and tour guide pass, I composed my response:

Do you want an honest answer? Never. Yes it fades but it will come back and visit again and again. Years will pass and you will still find the odd moment where tears come for seemingly no reason.

The first year is the hardest. All the firsts happen; first missed birthday; first Christmas; first anniversary. Once you make it to that, it gets easier. And the pain is more a loving remembrance. Which you will discover is a good thing.

You will miss her every day for the rest of your life. You will think of her every day. You will talk of her often. Let it happen. Don't let people tell you to get over it. Never let anyone take that away from you. She was your mom, after all. Remember her.

I didn't want to dress this up for you. I would be doing you a disservice. But the pain eventually gives way to an eternal love. I promise you.

If you ever need to talk, I will listen.

My friend appreciated the honesty and, also, the fact that I didn't try to "fix" her. I simply gave it to her as it is; a wound that never fully heals.

I would cross paths with my friend a few days later as I walked around a park at lunch. She was walking her dog and you could see it was an escape for her and a chance to decompress.

I walked up to her and said hi. She was happy to see me. I gave her a hug and said it was nice to see her again. What we had exchanged via email was left unsaid as we simply nodded in a moment of mutual understanding. I didn't need to say sorry as I could see she already knew and preferred me not to mention recent events in a public place.

After a few moments of weather talk, I departed from her to allow her to continue on the path, both figuratively and literally. If she needed me, I knew we would cross again. I had hoped for her that, someday, it would stop hurting so much.

ෆ

Ceilidh Surprise

I have told people to be aware of the "Strange things" that happen in the wake of a loved one's death. This consideration has evolved over time to become a message/messenger relationship; sometimes, the message is for you, and other times, you are the messenger.

Such a thing happened to me on the day of a friend's wedding. It was an auspicious day for me as, on my way to the church, I ripped the crotch out of my pants. Oh great, I thought, isn't this the most wonderful way to show up at a formal event; disclosing the colour of my underwear. Luckily for me, the wedding was in town and I could simply run home in the free time between the wedding and the reception to change my clothes.

The self-consciousness of sitting in a ceremony while being mindful of the possible exposure only seemed to heighten my intolerance for certain things because, as per Murphy's Law, the ceremony went longer than expected. I was sitting there, irritated that the priest bloviated into an audio distorting microphone. It reminded me of a typical comedy routine of a fast food drive thru. I am sure the priest had something valuable to say but the combination of the distortion of his voice and the thick accent made it seem like I was listening to an angry nest of bees rather than a homily.

My irritation was two-fold, however; I had this growing need to visit an Irish craft store in another part of the city. I'd only been there a couple of times in my life and never thought twice about it. But, for some reason, I felt this calling to go there. Why was that? It seemed, for some strange reason, I needed a necklace. I don't often wear jewelry so why the hell did I suddenly need a necklace? I have clothes that need changing! While air conditioning is appreciated on a warm day, such amenities are not desirable when it comes to pants in formal situations. Regardless, the need for a necklace from this particular store grew in consort with my irritation to leave this extended incomprehensible ceremony.

The irritation compounded as the lineup was slow to get out of the church. I am one of those types of people who feels the need to sit in the back of the church because, like a high school classroom, this is where all the cool kids sit. Sitting at the back means you get to be out the door first. A formal setting like a wedding is one of the times where the reverse is true because, first in front is the first out of the church. Sitting at the back means, in the orderly fashion of weddings, you are the last to leave.

The people in the aisle were slow to leave the church and my patience was approaching capacity. I could feel almost a desperate need to get to this store. The more obstacles placed in the way, the more the desire to get there. Why am I being delayed like this? And, why the hell is there such a desire in the first place? I don't need a necklace!

At this point, I don't know the "why" anymore and it ceases to matter; this is something I must do and something within me seems to know the answer, but it isn't telling. It almost had a cosmic mystery to it.

As I seemed to have a glacial amount of time with the current obstacles in my way, I thought about what type of necklace to get. My first goal was to get something that matched the Claddagh ring my dad gave me before he passed. So, a Claddagh necklace was the order of the day.

I was finally able to make it out of the church and drive across the city to the Irish store. It is located on a busy street with unfriendly parking. The store resembles a mom and pop shop and is used as a fund raising venue for the Irish community in the city. It is not a busy shop for much of the year and, when you walk in, it is normal to be the only customer in the store.

That is how I would find the place today. I walked in and it was quiet as usual. I awaited a greeting from a lonely or bored salesperson behind the counter. I often wondered how many books a person can read as a full time employee here because you could go hours between customers.

I would not be greeted by a lonely salesperson. Instead, a woman stood up, wiping her eyes and trying desperately to look presentable. She greeted me with a weak, "Can I...can I help you with anything?" She had been crying.

"Are you okay?" I said as I drew near to her. Several criminal scenarios played out in my head as to what caused her tears.

"Oh, I'm okay." she said, wiping her eyes some more, "I just got a call from my daughter and she gave me news I didn't want to deal with."

"Okay..." I said, trailing off but still concerned. The woman could see I was more concerned about her instead of shopping.

"No no!" she said, taking herself out of the moment, "It's okay, how may I help you?"

"I feel as though I should be helping *you*." I replied, feigning interest in the merchandise while measuring her emotional state.

I did my best to pretend to look like an interested customer but, I had a sudden realization as to why I was there. It explained the irritation, the sense of urgency. Was I being called to this woman? And, if so, who was submitting the request? Or is this just coincidence?

"Oh these?" she said, pointing at her puffy eyes, "These are tears of joy. Tears of joy! The Toronto Blue Jays just won for the first time in 17 games at Yankee stadium. I am happy they won!" She motioned to the radio which was supposed to validate her reason. Somehow, I was supposed to believe this radio had broadcast the game which had just ended; a radio that was silent when I entered the store.

"The Blue Jays won, eh?" I replied while cocking my head, "You must be a *big* fan!"

"Oh, that I am!" she said, laughing while blowing her nose.

The lady had a lot of wares in front of me to sell, but the one thing I wasn't buying was her act. I was compelled to press her because I felt this was the reason I was brought here. What did I have to lose? If she got mad at me and kicked me out, at least I didn't have to spend any money. I had nothing to lose and, when I find myself in those positions in life, I feel a freedom and bravery that other situations don't allow.

I looked at her, smirked, and said, "I will forgive your dishonesty."

We proceeded to go through the bow, curtsey and dance that a merchant and customer go through as I looked for a necklace. None of her wares appealed to me, but being the good salesperson she is, she kept finding me new amulets for me to consider. I finally settled on one that the woman said her daughter would have liked. That was good enough for me. For some reason, this necklace wasn't a piece of jewelry anymore as much as it was destined to be a souvenir of an imminent experience I anticipated.

It was time to get back to the issue at hand.

"You know, it's just you and me here. I am just a stranger and sometimes we just need to talk. What happened?"

I watched as this woman's guard came down. She couldn't pretend anymore; the jig was up. She looked down and replied, "My daughter just phoned to see if we were doing anything for my son's birthday. He died in February. This is the first birthday without him."

"Ah, the Year of Firsts!" I said as if it was some trademarked official stage of grief, "I've been there. First birthday is one of them; first birthday, first Christmas..."

The woman looked at me and I watched her defenses further reduce. Her body language showed she could trust me.

"That's right!" she said with a hint of surprise, "I told him not to buy that damned motorcycle." She then gritted her teeth and turned away.

"You just have to get to the first anniversary." I offered, "After that, it gets easier. Well, as 'easy' as they *say* it gets." I punctuated the sentence with an awkward laugh that oddly served to contradict and validate the statement at the same time.

Such is the nature of dealing with a death; the truth is an awkward journey of things that don't make sense in the now, and yet they *may* make sense at a later date. None of it, whether it makes sense or not, draws any comfort because no answer returns you to a whole person. This woman had the added burden of dealing with an incongruence of the natural order as children are not supposed to die before the parents.

As if being pushed, I continued to inquire: "What happened?" I found it odd that I didn't preface it with the phrase "If you don't mind me asking". There was already a perceived permission with the admission of the motorcycle.

"He was hit by a car." she replied, "He didn't die right away. He died ten months after the accident. He developed a disease, a cancer, in the aftermath of his injuries. I am pretty sure the two are related. I mean, he didn't have the cancer before his injuries and it appeared where all his injuries occurred."

I nodded and waited for her to continue.

"The person who hit him cut him off. My son was on the highway going highway speed when she made a left turn across the highway. She didn't see him and he didn't have time to avoid her."

She then paused and made fists with her hands, reimagining and reliving the day.

"And, this makes me so mad," she continued, "The person claimed she was 'New Canadian! New Canadian!' at the scene of the accident. Like that somehow gave her an excuse. She had an international driver's license.

"Are the rules different in other countries? How can she not see my son in broad daylight?"

I sighed and said words that jumped out of me like they weren't my own; "You have to forgive her."

"It was noon when she hit him!" she shot back, "How could she not see him?"

"It's easy," I confessed, "I know that stretch of highway and I did the same thing two decades ago. I made a left turn across that highway after a few cars had passed by and thought it was safe. It wasn't.

"As I turned across the lanes, an oncoming motorcycle seemed to come out of nowhere and nearly hit the back of my car. I am almost certain that, had he hit me, the cyclist would have died and that person's mother would be relaying this same story to some other stranger in another part of town. Maybe even right now as I stand before you. I could have been responsible for a death just like that 'new Canadian' was.

"I wasn't looking for a motorcycle," I continued, "I was looking for cars and trucks; bigger objects. I had a moment of failed judgment. Just like that 'new Canadian' with that international driver's license. My experience of living here all my life didn't stop me from having a careless moment; an almost fatal moment."

I could tell my story had hit home with her as she stood there for a moment and let my words sink in. Those words, that story, was meant for her to hear. It was meant to alleviate some of the anger she had been holding against that person. But, it wasn't quite enough.

"You wouldn't have tried to use an excuse like 'new Canadian' to try to get out of it." she countered as her fists clenched again, "That's what makes me so mad. There was no regret, no accountability on her part."

"You are talking to a person who lost his father to a mistake during a simple procedure in the hospital." I said, "I watched as nurses and a doctor lied and covered it up right in front of me. Just like that 'new Canadian' said desperate things, the hospital staff did desperate things. They didn't want to get into deep trouble even though it was already too late. It wasn't about them not caring; they were trying to save themselves without thinking about what they did. Desperation makes you do funny things.

"I have to find it in my heart to forgive that doctor and those nurses despite the lies and despite the cover-up."

"You shouldn't forgive them!" she countered, "The mistake itself you can forgive – those things happen; I was a nurse at one time – but the lying and the covering up? I wouldn't forgive that."

"I have not forgiven them yet." I replied, "I have to forgive it eventually; *all* of it."

"No you don't! Not all of it! Forgiving the mistake? Yes, I can understand that." she said as her emotions started to escalate, "Not forgiving would eventually eat you up."

I stopped and let the words hang in the air for her to catch them. She had answered her own objections. There was also no point in debating with someone who was still resolving unanswerable questions. A lot of times, in the midst of our grief, we have the answers for other people that are more applicable to ourselves. Our answers sometimes stare at us and we don't see them; like an oncoming motorcycle on a bright and clear day.

After a beat or two of silence, I fought back a resigned smile, nodded and said, "You're right; not forgiving would eventually eat me up."

I paid for my necklace and asked if I could give her a hug. She said yes and we embraced. I told her I was sorry for her loss. She replied that she was sorry for my loss as well. I was caught off guard by her sympathy for me because I felt this whole moment was for her. However, there was a lesson in this for me because I do not practice what I preach as far as forgiveness.

"My name is Joanne." she said, offering her hand. I shook it and told her my name. "This was really good. I'm glad you came in." She added with a smile as she wiped her eyes, "This was the best thing to happen to me all day." Her posture elevated and the darkness that I first saw in her lifted.

I smiled and turned for the door. I had a wedding reception to get back to, afterall! I stopped as I went to exit and called back to her, "Just so you know, this was no coincidence." Joanne gave a non-committal nod and went back to the cash register. I didn't know if the words would resonate with her right now. But, I figured they would eventually. In the present, she needed to absorb what just took place.

I returned to my car and had a moment of reflection. All those irritating delays in the church – the long homily, the slow lineup – allowed for a window where Joanne's daughter could phone prior to my arrival. Had I shown up at the store 20 minutes earlier without those delays, I likely buy my necklace and leave, never having had that conversation because I would not have found her crying. It would have been business as usual.

The timing of the events on this day can be explained away by chance and dumb luck. The burning desire to go to a store I have seen twice in my life, however, leaves me wondering how the idea came to me in the first place. Was all of it – the desire, the timing and the resulting conversation – just a cosmic roll of the dice? Or was it something else? Therein lie the questions to which I cannot answer with any degree of satisfaction.

At the very least, I have a souvenir necklace as a reminder of the encounter; a reminder that we eventually have to forgive lest we be "eaten up". It is my unintended amulet; my Ceilidh Surprise.

☙

Good Bye, Irene

Imagine walking into a theatre and witnessing only the final moments of a movie before the credits roll. Can you piece together the entire story with just the denouement? How would your story deviate from the actual events?

Such an opportunity presented itself to me on the scenic Iron Mountain Road in South Dakota. The highway is a "bucket list" drive I would recommend to anyone as it offers a variety of beautiful perspectives of Mount Rushmore as well as a few tunnels thrown in to keep your driving honest. There are plenty of opportunities to stop at designated areas and absorb the scenery. If you ever find yourself near Mount Rushmore in South Dakota, please do yourself a favour and locate this road. You will not regret it.

I had taken my parents here in 2008 after they were inspired by the photos I brought back earlier in the year. They had never left Canada for a vacation in their entire lives and I saw it as an opportunity to show them something different. I drove my parents all over the area and, as my instincts urged, I never allowed them to take the wheel once. "Just enjoy the scenery," I would say, "You don't see as much if you drive." I had assured my parents that I would return one day and can sightsee then. Right now, this trip is more for them than it is for me.

I also had a nagging suspicion about dad at the time because his throat had been bothering him. I had this innate desire to be the tour guide just in case it was the last time he would be here. As it turned out, my intuition would serve me well.

We took time out from the drive to stop at one of the many parking-friendly lookouts that adorned the Iron Mountain Road. This particular one was more elaborate than the others as it had formal lookouts with railings that allowed you to see the grand vista of the Black Hills. It was a perfect rest stop.

As we scouted around the area, I found myself leaning on the railings that faced towards Mount Rushmore. There was just something so peaceful and calming about the view. And, so clean!

"...Darcy." came a voice from behind me. It was my mom. I continued to gaze forward.

"...Darcy." my mom said again, this time sounding a little more insistent. I figured they spotted an animal they wanted me to see. But, as it turned out, they were alerting me to something different.

I turned and saw a middle aged man walking up to the railing. He was wearing, of all things, a Hawaiian button shirt and mismatching shorts. He wore a hat that seemed to cover what I would guess was a bad hair day. He was a walking fashion faux pas and I smirked as he approached. I could imagine that this gentleman was not a big hit at parties as he seemed to lack a lot of social grace.

I went back to engaging with the view when I heard the gentleman shake a bag beside me. He was dumping something over the railing and onto the ground. *What the hell was he doing? Littering? That son of a—*

As I turned to admonish this man, I saw what he was doing; he was spreading a small bag of ashes. On the bag, in felt marker, was scribed "Goodbye, Irene". He had a second bag with him, obviously meant for another place, which read "I love you, Irene".

I felt like a sudden interloper on a private moment and I stepped back to let him pay his respects. He finished spreading the ashes, stepped back from the railing, gave a nod with a satisfied smile, and took a picture with a cheap disposable camera. I thought the cheap disposable camera was perfect for a socially awkward man in a mismatching outfit. It gave a sense of consistency and seemed to fit with his character. Had he had an expensive camera, it would have been like a movie character breaking the fourth wall.

The gentleman turned and walked back to his car. There was a certain satisfaction in his step; the fulfillment of a promise. He was clearly on a mission to honour someone whom he considered special.

I stood there, stupefied, and left to ponder what had just happened. Who was Irene? A lover? A mother? A sister? A daughter? Just a really good friend? And, what brought about the end of her life? Those were just the initial questions. It was like uncovering the corner of a rock on a beach, only to realize there was much more underneath the sand, and you were going to require a shovel.

My parents and I would discuss the moment for the rest of the day and infrequently over the course of the next year. We had only witnessed the final chapter in Irene's existence, but she spoke to us through her anonymous loved one who, with mismatched clothes and a cheap disposable camera, ventured out here, away from civilization, to honour someone he felt deserved the time and the effort.

I am usually a curious sort, but in this case, there is a beauty in the mystery of this tale. I don't want to know the story. I don't need to know the story. The moment stands alone as the *entire* story. All the details I needed to know – love, honour, and a fulfilled promise – took place in the denouement I was privileged enough to stumble upon in this flowing, perpetual theatre that is life.

Roll credits.

The Lost Cherubs

Tragedy in one's life often does two things; it scars you but, it also blesses you. Such a statement might seem clichéd or counterintuitive, but that is the nature of life; stealing with one hand; giving with the other.

Such is what happened to my sister many years ago. Over a period of two years, she would experience three devastating miscarriages.

As a man, I won't ever fully understand the deepest, most intimate impact of such an event; I can only observe it and sympathize up to a certain point. I can see the scars but will never feel the physical and emotional depth.

However, it doesn't prevent me from understanding a healing that arrived through an "accident" of chance.

It was Christmas time in the year of my sister's third and final miscarriage. It had happened approximately 8 months previous, and it was the event where she decided that this was it; no more attempts to have children. She had one daughter at the time, and she figured that was enough. The three miscarriages after this daughter had taken their physical and emotional tolls. The third one almost cost her life because it was a tubal pregnancy that burst into her abdomen and would hospitalize her for about a week. She would lose one of her ovaries in the process and, therefore, significantly reduce her chances of getting pregnant again.

She was devastated. Of the three that she lost, two had been gestated enough that my sister knew that one was a boy and another was a girl. The third one, being tubal, had no human form and was only a cell cluster that burst the fallopian tube. She had no idea what sex the last one was but, she had names for them all. Names only she knows to this day.

The losses of these unknown children affected her deeper than I could ever relate. She went into depression and questioned her value as a woman because she was unable to reproduce. I can only guess that it is in a similar way an infertile man questions his societal worth. However irrational, she wondered what good she was now that she likely could never have more children.

After each adverse event, she would dust herself off and commit to raise her daughter. But she had this nagging feeling about the three she had lost. The trio felt like broken promises on a divergent path in her life that would forever remain unrealized.

As I said, it was the Christmas season and I was shopping in the mall. Because of the size of our family, we pulled names in those days so we didn't have to buy presents for everyone. I had someone else's name but, I came upon a gift that I felt was perfect for my sister. It was a poster that cost only three dollars. I thought to myself, "Oh, what the heck, why not get it for her?" My sister was a fan of the style, and there was no question in my mind that I had to get this for her. The poster had caught my attention for some unexplainable reason and it kept begging me to take it home like an anxious puppy from an animal rescue. I was dubiously compelled to get this extra gift and break the rule of pulling names.

It was a replica of an obscure Renaissance painting featuring three chubby little cherub angels. Two were facing forward while one appeared to be shying away, its head turned towards the other two with a hand up to the forehead to conceal the face:

Actual Painting

I'd not thought twice about it. This was my sister's style and something I thought she'd appreciate from an art perspective. I purchased it, took it home and wrapped it. This would serve as a birthday present in case I was playfully chided about breaking the rules of pulling names. I would forget about this gift until we visited her place during week leading up to the New Year.

When my sister opened the gift, she gasped. Spontaneously, another sister gave an enthusiastic, "Ooh! That's good luck for the new year!" The other sister didn't know what she had said at the time; it was something that just burst forth from her.

My sister absorbed the poster with a solemn stare – half stupefied and half reflective – and quietly rolled it back up. I didn't catch it at the time, but she was removed from the moment and transported somewhere else. She gave a measured thank you and held the roll like she had been given something both fearful and priceless. I had no idea what had just happened and continued with the evening unaffected and unaware.

It wouldn't be until weeks later that I would understand the gift's impact. My sister had placed the poster in a safe, secure place, and was planning on framing it. This was a basic, three dollar poster from a discount big box store! It was something most people stick pins through and hang in a play room until it becomes tattered at the edges and fades in the sunlight. It was, at its base, a disposable reproduction as there were thousands more of those posters in discount bins around the country. Its retail value wasn't even half of minimum wage at the time.

While I understood the poster's retail value, I didn't understand its intrinsic value. The moment my sister unrolled the poster and gazed upon it, she saw *her* three little angels – the children she had lost – staring back at her. One looked like a boy. One looked like a girl. And one was the face turned away, coy and shy.

My sister's first two miscarriages were developed enough to have a face. She knew the face. The third one was a cluster of cells; a face she never saw. By coincidence, the poster represented each and every one of them.

My sister had agonized over each of them, and every day, she pondered what might have been. Where were they? What were they doing now? Did they even go anywhere?

She just...wanted to know!

It's the kind of inquiry that sounds crazy to people who haven't walked that path. It was like her children were out there somewhere, alone in the streets – maybe in an alleyway – hiding from the strangers who come and go. They were afield, not being protected or loved. Worst of all, they were not at home safe with their mother.

If they existed, were they lost and longing for a place to call home?

With this simple, inexpensive poster, she felt an ease and no longer wondered. For, there they were, looking back at her through a poster. It was as if they were saying, "We're okay. We never wandered the streets alone. We are, and always have been, in a good place."

In the twinkling of an eye, she found peace, healing, and was able to move on with her life. She felt the roles had been reversed; that these children were now looking out for her. It was something that no family counsellor on earth had been able to give her.

She had traversed a dark and wide expanse of grief over these supposed "lost" children. During that time, she could see clear to the horizon of a desolate land all around her and was not able to reach a hand to the edge that could bring her out of it. In the midst of this landscape, it would be three simple images on paper that would manifest, reach into her, and transform the surroundings where the sun could rise again.

While her scars would remain to this day, they would cease to be open wounds intended to drain her. Rather, they are a sealed mark of honour in remembrance; memorials of a once and continued existence.

All this was delivered from a cheap, big box store Renaissance poster that insisted on a place to call home.

☙

My Perfect House

Lionel

"Hello, Darcy, this is Lionel of RE/MAX with your listings..." began the answering machine almost every day when I got home after work. It was this way every day since I hired the services of my Real Estate agent, Lionel. He would phone and leave me a message every day without fail while I was at work, and told of all the houses I may be interested in within my specifications. It was uncanny! I had never witnessed such a hard working agent in my entire life. He was determined to sell me what I described to him as my perfect house.

I wasn't looking for a mansion; just a place to call home. I didn't have a lot of money at the time, and I had saved up for 5 years to bank enough for a down payment. I didn't want any help from my parents as it was important for me to do this on my own. Besides, my parents were not in a position to help buy me a house anyway.

The messages on my answering machine were like a welcome home every day. As I was living alone at the time, Lionel was becoming a familiar greeting I had become accustomed to and had started to expect. It had gotten to the point where I looked forward to hearing Lionel's voice as he tirelessly listed house after house that had come on the market that day. *Did he do this for every one of his other clients?* I would think. Turns out, the answer was yes; every single one of his clients got this treatment. The amount of energy required for this repetitive, time consuming task seemed staggering to me. I was a simple office worker in a simple job at the time; I did not have the ambition and the energy that Lionel had; not even close!

The Perfect Agent

While Lionel was ambitious, he never compromised his honesty. He never showed you a house that he knew would not be compatible. He never tried to sell you on something that wasn't a fit. When you looked at a property, he would give you a brutal and honest assessment.

I remember one house we viewed; the exterior looked fantastic and I was excited. However, this evaporated when we went into the basement. I saw the deflected interior walls and noted the shifts in the foundation. I was waiting for Lionel to sell me on the idea of this house. Just some beams and elbow grease ought to fix that up, right?

"Well, so much for this house," Lionel said to me, "I guess we keep looking." He shrugged and we left the house.

As I walked back to my car, I had to inquire: "There's nothing fixable about that house? You mean...?" I was testing him to see if he would put a pretty bow on a money pit.

"That's a terrible house for you, Darcy." replied Lionel, "You will waste a lot of time and money fixing that place. I won't sell it to you. We will find one; there are others." He gave a reassuring smile and touched my shoulder in a casual manner as he headed to his car. It was no big deal; there are other houses.

I had heard so much about Lionel. He was a legend in the city for his honesty and his dogged determination to find you exactly for what you were looking. Your happiness appeared to be his happiness.

I knew I had the right agent.

Lionel...?

I had spent a couple of months with Lionel as we looked at house after house, none was to my appeal. I was starting to feel like I was wasting his time. Lionel never let on that I may be a difficult client and always, without fail, left me a phone call every week day. He would still take me to all the houses I wanted to see with the same enthusiasm as he had done on our first day. I was impressed how he could exercise such patience with me.

We had a few adventures while looking at houses. I remember one night, he had accidentally set off the security alarm on this one house and couldn't get it to disarm. It bellowed throughout the neighbourhood and announced our presence with the grace and elegance of an angry bull at a rodeo. "Ah, shit!" he said as he rushed to his mobile phone and frantically called people to make it stop. It was the only time I had heard him swear and it made me smile. I also thought it might be funny to have a police escort for the viewing. That would have been a first for all of us, I am sure!

As the weeks passed, I started to notice that Lionel wasn't as responsive to me anymore when we looked at houses. He seemed distracted and disengaged at times. The last house we looked at, he opened the front door, sat in the porch, and just told me to go in and look on my own. It was an odd behaviour from Lionel and a complete disembarkation from his character. Was he sick of me? Did he give up on me?

I looked through the house and came back to the porch. Lionel was slumped over and breathing heavy.

"Lionel...?" I said, concerned, "You okay, man?"

"Oh, I'm fine," he replied, his voice weaker than normal, "It just happens sometimes. I'm fine."

"Okay..." I said, reluctant to engage him, "You sure you're okay?"

"Oh, it's probably just a cold. You know this time of year." he replied as he laboured to get up from the bench and walked to his car. As much as we both tried to downplay this moment, it gave me concern.

For some reason, I didn't quite buy the story he was selling. For the first time in our relationship, it appeared Lionel lied to me.

Silence

That would be the last time I would see Lionel. The once-a-day phone messages would become every second day, then every third. His voice sounded more and more like he had been talking through fabric and, some of his messages were the satirized versions we often hear of drive through speakers.

The frequency increased where I would get home from work, and the light on my message machine would be still; no messages. The loudest sign something was amiss occurred when two weeks of conspicuous silence would pass.

Was he mad at me?

I decided to phone the agency to inquire as to his whereabouts. The front office staff would answer:

"May I speak to Lionel please? I am his client, Darcy Donovan."

"Oh, thank you for phoning, Darcy." she said with a tone that seemed off, "I will patch you through to our manager."

Manager? What? Had I done something wrong? Did my agent fire me and not tell me?

"Hello, Darcy? I understand you are a client of Lionel's?"

"Yes, I am. I've not heard from him in a couple of weeks. I would like to know if I can talk to him."

"Well, Darcy, I hate to break this news but Lionel is very sick, and he is in Palliative care right now." said the Manager, "We understand that he is likely not to make it and they are just keeping him comfortable now. He is surrounded by family and they are making sure his needs are taken care of. That's all they can do."

After a beat or two of silence to absorb what I just heard, I blurted out, "You can't be serious!"

"I wish I wasn't," said the manager as his voice trailed off, "We can certainly let you know should there be any...developments."

"I would appreciate that," I said, knowing full well what "developments" meant, "Um...thank you. I think." I gave a nervous laugh. It just seemed to be the only way to punctuate it.

As I hung up the phone, each piece of evidence over the past few weeks now became abundantly clear. Each sign settled upon my heart and weighed it down in my chest. Dammit, I would have preferred Lionel had fired me. This just wasn't right; a good man like that isn't supposed to die. It wasn't fair.

Despite all his relentless efforts and the Patience of Job, Lionel was not going to sell me my perfect house.

The Funeral

The phone call would come a short time later. Lionel had passed away peacefully at home with his family at his bedside. The only thing I was thankful for was that his suffering was brief. He was a good and honourable man and he appeared to have departed in an honourable way.

At the funeral, I would discover the true value of a person in this life as I was forced to park more than four crowded blocks away from the church to attend the service. I had been lucky enough to sit in the back lobby by the door with a peek-a-boo view of the service through an open door in the antechamber. The entire basement of the church – a large church – had been handling the overflow crowd as they had to watch the service on closed circuit TV.

This...this is the measure of a man! I thought to myself, *It is not the materials you accumulate; it is the lives you've touched.*

Lionel apparently touched more than anyone I have ever known. I listened to the eulogy to find a man of a strong Christian faith who didn't preach to people, but lead by example. There was a story of him excusing himself from his group of friends in a coffee shop to sit with a man who was obviously hurting and down on his luck. Lionel had bought his meal and offered him some money to get through the day. He treated the least our brothers in the same way he treated his clientele.

These are things I didn't know about Lionel. He was just a hard working agent to me. I respected him as a professional. But now, I have had the opportunity to love him as a person; a person whose departure made the world poorer, but in contrast, his legacy made everyone else he touched richer. He is one person who clearly left this existence better than when he found it.

As I walked four blocks back to my car after the service, I pondered the man now gone. I knew Lionel for a bare four months before his passing, and yet he took up enough space to create an absence; he also was the source of an unfulfilled promise.

The Dream

Months would pass. I didn't take on a new agent as no one seemed to measure up to Lionel. I was also heartbroken and didn't know it. Why do good people die so early? He was only 50.

The money I had saved for a down payment on a house just didn't matter for the time being. Should I just blow it on a vacation? New Zealand is a place I've not seen. Maybe I should just take the money and go there for a couple of weeks. Apartment life isn't so bad, now, is it? I can live there forever, I guess. Besides, who is going to have the patience that Lionel had? I was a first-time home buyer and a fussy one at that.

About a year after the funeral, the dust had settled on the whole issue. I didn't blow the money on a vacation. I was going to save it and get a house...eventually. But who was going to sell me my perfect house?

It was about that time that I had an unusual dream.

I dreamt that I was with Lionel and he was showing me one more house. It appeared to be winter as we walked to the property. It seemed to have a rather large garage. Wow, how could I afford this? We'd go check it out anyway.

The dream cuts to the kitchen. It looks okay. It is pedestrian and normal by my standards. I shrug and say it is okay. We only spend a few moments here, and then we leave.

We then move to the living room. It is dark and no light can penetrate to the end of it. I see a few light fixtures but they are not lit. There is also no furniture in here and the colours are grayscale. It feels cold in this room, and we don't spend long here either.

The dream then cuts to the basement. This basement has seen better days. It had beams holding up the walls and I was lead to a corner where the floor had sunken in and there was gravel coming up through the foundation. I found this to be rather odd. Usually, Lionel would have marched me out of the house and said to forget it.

I motioned to the rubble in the sunken corner and asked, "Does this affect the value of the house?"

Without skipping a beat, Lionel waves his hand to cancel out my thought. "Don't worry about it." he said. It was definitive; don't question it.

The answer struck me as odd. But, I trust Lionel and will go with his opinion and advice.

The dream then cuts back to the kitchen. It has changed. The colours are brighter than before; the kitchen table is a beautiful oak I'd not noticed the last time; there is also a bright chandelier now here! Where did *that* come from!

I look out the window of the kitchen and there is a bright light peering in. It was like the sun but it appeared to be reaching towards me. This light brought me to a calm and the air felt fresher.

I think I found my perfect house!

"How about I offer them 69 (thousand) for it?" I said to the open air. After all this time, I had *finally* been comfortable enough to put an offer on a house. I was comfortable with this. It felt good.

I turned to look at Lionel. He was sitting at the kitchen table. He smiled, leaned back in the chair, and lifted his hands behind his head, reposed. A bright glow emanated from him; his mission of selling me a home had been accomplished.

I did a double-take on the image of Lionel. While it seemed glorious, it seemed out of place and odd. Looking back, the oddest part of the dream was that I didn't react in awe.

The dream then cuts to Lionel and myself, walking side by side as we return to our cars. He is motioning his hand like he is talking to me. He is relaying information to me that I can't hear but I desperately want to pull out of the dream.

The dream ends.

The Dream Persists

I awoke that day feeling refreshed and energy abundant. I didn't know why, but for some reason, I felt great and at peace all day. I was happy to talk to my coworkers and was pleasant even in the face of the daily grind. Nothing bothered me over that period of time, and I felt nothing but a resonating peace. This seemed to come out of nowhere and I didn't make the connection between the dream and my newfound attitude.

That is, until two weeks later.

The dream lingered with me like a psychological afterimage; like when your eye persists to see something long after the flash of the original image has ceased; it appears every time you blink. My state seemed to thrive off this; the dream, along with its vivid details, would not evaporate. Instead, it endured and drew attention every day. It was calling me to look closer.

I was at work one day, email chatting with my friend, Jackie. Jackie and I have an unusual friendship in that, on paper, it normally would never have been possible for our paths to cross, let alone remain friends. She was a country gal who trained horses for a living. She was a tough, no bullshit woman who almost always shot from the hip. The dichotomy that lives within of Jackie is that she was also a model in Japan earlier in her life. She had lived both ends of the spectrum; a glamourous city life and, now, a simple yet tough country life.

I met Jackie back when we both worked at a telecommunications company. She was in my department and we worked on a few projects together. When I left the company, we kept in touch through email. This would endure to the present day and, sometimes, years would pass between us meeting in person. I sometimes wonder how this friendship has survived, and maybe it is because we can talk about anything to each other.

Jackie is someone who is in touch with her deeper side. She is not religious but more deeply spiritual. She gets it from all the time she spends outdoors with her horses. I guess you could say she has the spirituality of a cowgirl; where the land is the cathedral by which we are all placed to fulfill a Devine Purpose. Her vision of the world is complimentary to mine, and maybe that's why we can discuss deeper things and learn from each other. I can be honest and say that I've never had a boring conversation with her.

On this day, Jackie and I were going through the motions – Your boss is being an ass? Mine too! Time to get my lottery ticket and punch out of this workaday life! – when I finally just wrote, "Okay, so, I had this dream a couple of weeks ago and it's just stuck with me. Do you interpret dreams?"

Jackie responds: "No, I've never interpreted a dream before but, what the hell, send it to me and let's see what I can come up with."

I sent Jackie the details. The following response is the actual email with Jackie's interpretation in italics. It would leave me gob smacked:

The Interpretation

My real estate agent (who passed away last spring) is showing me my "perfect" house. He is walking me through every room and the layout of the house is okay, not perfect by my standards but, still, I'm happy with it. I remember being very happy just walking with him through the home. It was a very warm feeling.

I am aware that he has been dead for many months but somehow it's like he isn't gone, like it never happened. He shows me the kitchen, which is the first room in the house. We had to walk up a flight of "naked" wooden stairs from outside (by that, I mean, it was just the stair frame with a wooden railing like old houses have in their basement). We had to walk through the garage for some reason to get to these stairs to enter the home.

Ok, this is your classic past/present/future scenario. Walking up the stairs into the garage is transferring into the netherworlds of what is to come. The house is 'perfect' because it is the house of 'you'.

The kitchen has a nice view over the street has a nice dark wooden trim much like the exterior of a Dutch style home. There is a nice bright white light coming in from the kitchen windows and it is fully furnished with kitchen table, chairs, stove, etc. The kitchen table set is VERY NICE in that it is one of those expensive dark woods. I am very happy with the kitchen.

> *The kitchen is the present. If is full and bright and you are contented and comfortable there.*

There is a narrow passage way to the living room at the back of the house. This room is a lot darker than the kitchen and I can't see to the end of the room. There are no lights and no furniture in the room. We just basically look in for a few seconds and move on.

> *This room is the future. It is dark because it hasn't been created yet. There are no lights and no furniture because the future is yours to build. The endless expanse of the room is the endless possibilities of what you can do in your life.*

The dream cuts to the basement, which is unfinished. For some reason I'm not entirely thrilled with the basement but, again, it's passable. There is no furniture down there and I notice the walls are steel reinforced. We walk to a far corner of the basement where the floor is worn away and there is gravel. It looks as if there are some structural problems. Lionel (my agent) has his back to me as he leads me to the corner. I asked him if that was a huge issue with buying the house and he basically says, "Don't worry about it". I'm very comforted by that statement. Lionel seems very fatherly at that moment.

> *The basement is your past. There are some things about your past that you are not happy with. The steel reinforcements are the trials and tribulations that you have 'suffered' and represent the barriers that you have erected to shield yourself from 'structural damage'. The floor is worn because you have tread here; it is the past. You are asking Lionel if there is a problem with your past that will affect your future, Lionel reassures you that you have nothing to worry about.*

The dream cuts back to the kitchen and I'm again in front of the stove, looking at the windows overlooking the street. Again, there is a bright white light coming in from the street and I can't really make out what it is like outside. I am very comfortable with my surroundings and I now notice more of the tapestry in the kitchen. I can't believe I didn't notice these things before. There is now a beautiful wrought iron chandelier over the kitchen table and there are now plants where I didn't think there were plants before. Because of all this, I've made a decision to buy the house, just like that; even though the layout isn't perfect.

> *The white light is the essence of God showing you that he is always with you. Again you are comfortable in the present. After exploring your past,*

you are able to see new things about the present and you have decided that you can make peace with them (buy the house, even though the 'layout isn't perfect').

I say, "How about I offer them 69 for it?"

I look back to Lionel, who is sitting on a kitchen chair to my right near the entrance to the living room. He is surrounded by white light, which is blurring the details of his outline and face. He has his hands behind his head in a relaxed, reposed position, and from what I can tell, he is smiling.

Your offer to buy shows your commitment to accept the past, and the imperfections in yourself. Lionel is a messenger from God, an Angel.

The dream cuts to us on the street walking back to his car. It is a nice winter day as there is snow on the ground. I can only see his torso but his hands are motioning like he is explaining all I need to know to buy the house. I can hear him speaking but I cannot recall what he told me. I take note of the plaid shirt he is wearing because it seems so odd that he would wear that...it was black with the plaid parts being green. I remember thinking that's what my dad would wear. I feel a sense of peace.

Your angel explains all you need to be 'you'. You are not meant to remember what he said as the words enter your subconscious for future reference when you start to doubt yourself and your path. This is what gives you peace.

Gob Smacked

I am certain that, if someone were to witness me reading Jackie's reply, they would have seen my jaw slowly drop agape. I did not expect that answer at all. Not in a thousand lifetimes! And, yet, there was the naked truth staring back at me on the screen, reaching in and exposing all that is me in one page of on-screen text.

I knew the interpretation was the truth. It was undeniable. We all battle with the acceptance of self, don't we? It explained why I was in a good mood after the dream. It explained why it persisted; why it followed me sunrise to sunset each and every day since I dreamt it.

Everything was explained in one email reply from a person who claimed to know nothing about dream interpretation. Beginner's luck?

I felt like I had been stripped naked where I sat. I was at work and I needed to get out of there. It was mid-afternoon and my day was done. A blast wave was sweeping through my mind, obliterating anything work related in its path. My productivity was going to be nonexistent for the rest of the day.

I just needed to get home. I just needed to get home. I just needed to get HOME!

I replied to Jackie with: "Thank you! I was not expecting that. I just thought I was hanging out and spending time with Lionel. Thanks!" It was the best I could do as my psyche was starting to break down. I could feel the walls tumbling and I needed to dash and get somewhere where I could be alone.

I grabbed my coat and took the stairwell out of the building. I didn't want to cross paths with anyone and have to explain my early exit. I didn't want to answer questions. I had but one goal; HOME!

When I reached my car, I fought to put the keys in the ignition. "Why did you do this to me Lionel?" I said out loud, "Why did you do this to me?" It was almost like I was blaming him for my good mood the past two weeks.

I drove home through watered eyes. I was glad traffic was light because I was operating a vehicle with modest attention as my mind was somewhere else.

Just...get...home...

Sold...Finally

Once home, I sat on my couch for an undetermined amount of time and pondered my existence. I guess I had been hard on myself for much of my life. I held myself to standards that were designed for failure. I would use it as an excuse to affirm my lack of worth – *See? I knew you'd fail!* I guess I never fully accepted all that is me.

Well, apparently, not until now.

I thought it was just a silly dream. Who could have guessed that it had a multi-layered meaning? Not me, obviously!

In it is the message for all of us; does our past affect our value now and in the future? Are we worth less because of it?

When you ask yourself that question, imagine the definitive wave of a hand and a voice that says with conviction, "Don't worry about it." Leave your past, return to your present, and put an offer on yourself; accept yourself, steel beams, sunken floor, and all.

What he was unable to accomplish during his life, Lionel, tireless agent, had finally found a way to sell me my perfect house, and I am happy in my home. Thank you, Lionel!

ଓଃ

Renovated

Buffalo Pound

I went out to Buffalo Pound Provincial Park this day. It had been awhile since I last went to the buffalo lookout where my dad's ashes were spread. I hadn't had that "alone" time up there in a long time and, lately, I have felt a need to talk to him. This is my therapy whether he exists to listen to my monologues or not.

I explained to him everything that is occurring right now; How my siblings continue to not support like they should; How I feel like everything has been left on my shoulders; How mom needs to find a new place because of the second hand smoke and destructive gossip in her building; How I feel a lot of anxiety for the things I have been left to look after. I told him that I am feeling beaten up over things I didn't create *again* and just needed to talk about it.

As always, I knew dad couldn't come back from the dead and set things right. I knew no one could come out of the clouds, wave a magic wand and make everything better. If anything, these are just my personal crazy venting sessions that seem to have no rhyme, reason or purpose.

I then asked, hey, if there's anything you can do to give me a sign or tell me something, now is the time. I am in need of some encouragement right now. I left the request hang on the air and felt that, this was likely going to be it for the day.

Open Houses

I returned to Regina with the intent of seeing some open houses. It was a spontaneous idea and, as the home buying process has been nothing short of frustrating with the lack of quality, I fully expected this to be an exercise in futility.

I came upon a house in my old Regina neighbourhood in Cathedral Village. It had been once owned by an old friend back in the day. She had sold it to someone years ago and, I heard the place had undergone extensive renovations. When I saw there was an open house, how could I resist the temptation? Of course I couldn't!

It was a pleasant surprise to see the house I'd not seen the inside in almost 5 years or more. It had undergone extensive – and expensive – renovations. It now looked great. Not $317,000 great. But, still, pretty great. It was just a 700 square foot home! How can one justify the price?

I asked the agent why the house was so pricey. He said, well, there was an appraisal. I responded that appraisals are opinions and that I can still get something bigger and better for this price. He agreed. He then said, well, there was this house a block over on McTavish that sold for over $339,000 a few months ago.

I laughed and said, "Was it 2199 McTavish?" It was an inside joke meant just for me. I thought I was pretty clever and I took a moment to soak in my brilliance.

He responded that, yes, it was.

"You can't be serious!" I said, thinking that this would have been the perfect moment for one of those comedic spit-takes. "I was joking when I said that."

I continued, "That was my old house I sold back in 2011. There's no way in hell it's worth $339,000!"

The agent insisted that was the price for which my old house sold. "Would you like to see the photos?" he said, handing me his smart phone.

What I would see would render me silent. I am not one to be rendered speechless. But, today, I got to see what the people did to my house after I sold it in 2011.

My First House

I bought the place back in September of 2003 with a sense of promise. That house meant a lot to me. It was my first house and, I still remember how I walked around it after the agent handed me the keys, signed off, and left. I was saying, "This is mine? This...is *mine*!" It was a moment 5 years in the making because I started from scratch and saved the money for the down payment. I had refused help because this was something I had to do on my own. A long and often frustrating journey had reached its end goal. Now was the time to celebrate a successful venture.

The very first thing I brought into the house was a crucifix. I went through every room of the house, blessed it and asked for peace, success and prosperity in this home.

This is MY HOUSE! My house? Yes! My house!

It didn't quite feel real...until my first guests arrived 45 minutes later. They were my mom and dad. I remember how proud I was to hold the door open for them and say, "Welcome to *MY HOME!*" and, I hugged my mom and shook my dad's hand as they entered. They were proud of me, I could feel it.

While scrolling through the present day photos, it dawned on me that the next time I would hold my dad's hand would be less than 7 years later as he drew his final breaths. Dad was not one for such emotional displays; even a heartfelt handshake from his own son. This moment was significant.

The house would evolve into a gathering place for family once a year during the Labour Day weekend. It's just something that happened. As it turned out, it was an event that people valued. Even though my houseguests would trash my place after those weekends and, it would take me all week to get it back to normal, it was fulfilling to bring people together. The house was serving a purpose for which it wasn't originally intended. And, it was great!

I would live almost the entire decade of my thirties there. Jobs and girlfriends came and went. Life's regular mix of the beautiful, the unfair and the teachable would unfurl as it does for everyone. It was, literally, the best of times and the worst of times.

Over the final 2 years of my time there, the house would fall into disrepair and neglect. My father's needs replaced my own and I ended up quitting my job to help look after him until his untimely passing in 2010. My house just...wasn't a priority anymore. There was so much I wanted to do with it. There was so much I wanted to fix. I wanted to turn that place into something special but, my neglect meant that I had to put buckets in places around the house every time it rained. The grass would go uncut for weeks at a time. The house was now...just too much. And, mirroring my life at the time, the house was falling apart. I had to let it go.

Just like I had to let go of my job.

Just like I had to let go of my dad.

The Renovations

I ended up selling the house to people who promised to fix it. I would drive by every now and again and watch the changes take place. I could never quite see inside the house but, it looked like they had repainted the living room. I wondered if they kept the textured wall in the dining area. I wondered what they did about the slope in the porch. I wondered if they fixed the roof where all the leaks took place.

I would hear through others that, the house had flooded two months after I sold it. The timing, for me, was impeccable. The timing for the new owners? Not so much. I wondered how they dealt with that and, if it affected the foundation at all.

I would eventually see the house go from white exterior to green. They added cement railings on the front step and added a carport in the back. I couldn't quite tell what they did to the backyard as they had upgraded the fence.

The house was looking good; better than when I had owned it. It looked like some simple renovations that anyone could do with time and money. Or, so I thought.

The Reveal

I did not expect to see what I saw when I scrolled through those pictures. The interior was unrecognizable! The kitchen was gutted and replaced with high-end appliances. The textured wall that I loved so much was demolished to open up the entire main area. I didn't even miss that wall as, what had replaced it was, for me, jaw dropping.

I never had the money to repair the fireplace in my house. In the entire 7 years I lived there, I was never able to use it once. I had always wanted to. The closest I came was when I put a small TV in there and played the Yule Christmas Log DVD on repeat. That was my fireplace.

What exists there now is a rebuilt, modern fireplace. One that...it must have been expensive! Where did they get this thing? It is classy and feels homey all at once.

The backyard, once an undeveloped, open expanse of untamed yard that I cursed every time it started to grow out of control, was now a beautifully landscaped work of art with multiple levelled decks. It was a welcoming space that was perfect for entertaining. Now...*this* is what I could have used for those Labour Day Weekend parties!

The Message

The place...is...*BEAUTIFUL*! It has not only been restored, it has been made into everything I wanted it to be and much, much more! I scrolled through the photos, experiencing a sense of bittersweet joy. A flood of memories of what was and what could have been rendered me silent. I fought back tears as each new and ever jaw dropping photo revealed itself to me.

It was then that I felt what seemed like a telepathic finger touch upon my heart that said: *"...this is your message...*

"You will be redeemed and made better than you ever were."

The house that was mirroring my life was now showing me that something in disrepair can be fixed; that something that was not working can be renovated; that something that was once neglected can be redeemed and made better than it ever was. Sometimes, it just needs to be surrendered in the trust that the promise will be fulfilled.

It was at that moment, it all hit me: I surrendered a career that was limping at the time of my dad's illness, and a year later, that career was renovated and made into something better than it ever was. It is affording me opportunities to speak to people in forums I never knew existed. It seems this renovated career may spill over into my personal life and redeem it as well. In time, I will know.

As I finished scrolling through the pictures, I fought to keep myself composed in front of this stranger. *It's just a house, dammit! Why this reaction over a damned house?* I thanked him for his time. He offered to send me the link to the photos. I politely declined and told him I could get it from my agent. I just wanted to get out of there before I lost my composure. Besides, the agent's message was delivered and my connection to him was fulfilled.

I would return to my car and, a moment later, would be overtaken by tears. Not sad tears; revelatory tears; tears that spoke of how I felt unworthy of renovation and redemption. Tears that also spoke of a Greater Power that sent a message of unconditional love and how, no matter how much you reside in disrepair, that there is a way back for everyone. You can not only be repaired; you can be renovated.

Epilogue

In the days that followed this event, my mom would get a phone call for an affordable place to rent. The place was something she liked and was excellent on her budget. She could live here but also have a sense of community with other people in the building. It seems like a good place.

Three weeks later, on a half-hearted whim that I decided would be the last place I would browse until spring, I came upon a condo that would fulfill my needs. I remember distinctly, as I stood in the living room when I first saw the condo; I saw a Cabela's sign glowing into the living room. I found myself bowing my head and finding peace in the moment. My dad's favourite store in the world was Cabela's. It took me back to a trip we had taken years ago – his last – where, for a change, I was the one waiting for *him* with a tried patience in the store.

It seems like this was a message and an approval that *"This is the one"*.

I would put an offer on the condo and, after some back and forth, it was accepted. I would move into my new home 5 weeks later. The place, while more than I wanted to spend, feels like home.

Now, every evening I spend in my home, there is the gentle glow of a fond reminder illuminating my living room. It brings me a sense of peace.

ಌ

Sunset

In the summer of 2014, my mother and I visited the haunts of my youth; Cypress Hills Provincial Park in Southwestern Saskatchewan. We hadn't been there in over a decade and it was a chance to stir awake long packed away memories and witness how the park has changed, and stayed the same, in the years since our last visit.

Cypress Hills was one of my dad's favourite vacation spots. Not because it was a popular destination; but, because a portion of the park was left to nature, and if you decided to camp there, you were "roughing it". I remember how we tented in a designated spot where our shower, bath, and dishwasher was the ice cold stream near us and the bathroom was a classic outhouse. Those were the "amenities" in this land that regular tourists never dared seek.

I had often joked with my parents that we camped in places where "nobody can hear you scream" because we were miles from anyone and anything that resembled civilization. We would often hear wildlife trundling through our campsite at night, and sometimes you could tell they were *big*. Too big!

I was a city kid back then who had no use for such experiences. I wanted to be in the Centre Block of the park – the civilized part – where all the cool kids vacationed. They had cabins, stores, a calm man-made lake, and a pool. I wanted to frolic with friends and meet girls. I was incompatible with the outdoor lifestyle at the time and had no use for it. Why in the hell would one want to come out here in the deserted West Block when there were people, parties, and *actual* fun in Centre Block? Out here, it was like that joke of paying money to live like a homeless person. Most often, I would count down the days until the camping "adventure" ended and I could go home where there was TV and a hot shower. There was even one week we had spent in West Block where it rained nearly every day and we almost didn't make it out of the park because the roads were too muddy. This is something that wouldn't have happened at Centre Block because, you know, the roads were *paved* there!

Those rugged involuntary memories are a part of me now. While I didn't appreciate it at the time, I have grown to see what my dad saw in these parts; the beauty, the peace, and the quiet. I am more still and less restless inside now that I'm older, and I now take the time to let a place speak to me; I have developed the sense to listen.

Such is what happened one night at Lookout Point.

Lookout Point is one of the highest points in Saskatchewan. It has an easy access road and boasts one of the widest, most distant vistas in the province. It is a beautiful place that I remember fondly then, and now that I have returned, that fondness has grown and matured. On this night, I embraced the landscape through the same eyes I did as a child and am in the same awe as I was when my eyes were new. The place still transforms me from the talkative know-it-all into an awed, silent admirer. I guess that's what makes this place special, and if you are ever in Saskatchewan, it is a "bucket list" destination.

One evening, after a wildlife reconnoiter through the park, my mother and I decided to catch the sunset at Lookout Point. It felt like a race against time as, from our vantage point, the sun seemed to be in the initial phases of twilight. I would push the car as fast as I dared on the winding roads to reach the lookout.

Once there, we had discovered the sun was still above the horizon and we could still catch the show. There were a few familiar people there whom we had crossed paths with earlier on a day tour of nearby historic site, Fort Walsh. All of us stood on the rim of the lookout and watched a clear evening dissolve into a clear night.

Something was different about this sunset, though. All sunsets are gorgeous, but this one spoke to me more than the thousands of others that have taken place over my lifetime. The Sun floated, timeless and eternal, before a slow melt into the horizon. It splashed various flavours of light into the atmosphere; colours that made a splendorous crescendo as they sank back down into the civil twilight. Like a last dying ember, a pin of light held for longer than I've ever seen, raging against the dying of the light. I felt a connection to this pinpoint; a defiant farewell to the day. But it held; it held with a might and determination. And as it held its stare, it drew my attention ever greater and connected me to it as if there was an umbilical cord. You could say I bonded with this light as if it had been given life.

And, then it was gone.

I felt a strange disconnect when the pin of light winked out of existence. I stood there, feeling the moment empty out of me like water out of a punctured bucket. There was an odd feeling of loss.

Then I looked above the horizon and watched the nautical twilight. The pin of light was replaced with a halo; the afterglow of a day gone by. I found a strange comfort in the glow and smiled. It was a perfect sunset.

As I drove back to the campsite, the moment hung with me like a prolonged final note of a concerto, and it would stay with me for a long time afterwards.

I've often read endless accounts of a sunset being a metaphor for death but, never have I experienced it in this way. It reminded me of how one dies; how some of us linger and have that one dying ember holding on almost in defiance; the raging against the dying of the light; and then it is gone. However, as the intense light winks out, there is a soft halo; a gentle remembrance of all that was you.

This metaphor can be seen in two ways. In the worldly sense, the halo would be all that you left behind in terms of people who still talk about you; your light eventually gives way to darkness – when no one speaks of you or remembers your name – and you are truly gone. In the spiritual sense, it is like you crossed over to shine light on an unseen land; the eventual darkness is merely your being home with The One. And in some beliefs, you live again the next morning when the sun rises.

Whatever truth is weaved into the symbolism is not ours to know until we, too, are down to our own pin of light. Maybe our existence ends when the halo is gone and the astronomical twilight gives way to midnight black. Maybe we venture beyond the horizon and shine light onto an alien land where others are watching us rise and welcome us into a new day. How to prove either resides in mystery; a beautiful mystery that beckons at every day's end, leaving us to ponder our existence and our place on this side of the horizon.

༃

No Regrets

You never know when a "snippet of life" moment is going to fall upon you; sometimes it impacts you like a comet plunging into a planet. One would happen on New Year's Eve at the Moose Jaw Warrior Hockey Game.

There was always an elderly couple that sat beside us this season. They were such a cute couple; Ron and Eleanor. They were a friendly couple who befriended us the very first game and, mom and I always looked forward to going to games to see them again. Their antics were adorable; Ron would always cheer for the opposing team, no matter who it was, just to "spite" Eleanor. This would create a friendly rivalry every game and, with the Warriors being a sub .500 team this year, Ron would inevitably become "victorious" every game despite the irony of him wearing Moose Jaw Warrior paraphernalia. If the visiting team would score, Ron would clap and cheer while Eleanor would playfully hit and tell him to shut up. Even though the Warriors were having a terrible season and it was frustrating to watch, this couple gave us reason to smile and enjoy coming to games.

These was the signs of a beautiful, long lasting love that had reached a mature stage; where each other's "aroundness" was all that was needed to have a good time. It was a thing of beauty to witness.

This night, Ron would come by himself and announced to us that his wife had passed just 48 hours previous. He had said, one day, she was fine and, the next, she had pains in her abdomen. And, 10 days later, she was gone.

"I am so sorry, Ron," I said as I reached over and touched his arm. He gave a simple acknowledgment and a nod. You could see that the events of the past two weeks for him were still incredulous and had not quite registered as fact.

We had gotten around to the usual questions of how did she die and her age. He said it had been a cancer that didn't show its face until it was too late. And, she was 77. Ron then announces that he is also 77 but, six months younger.

"She liked her men younger and good looking!" he declared with a proud smile. And, we laughed.

Ron continued: "Not like you," he says, pointing at me, someone three decades his junior, "You're looking pretty old. Not young and spry like me!"

I couldn't hear him over the public address announcer and I asked him to repeat himself.

He motioning to my mom and says, "See? His hearing's gone." And, we laughed again.

Amidst all this laughter, my mom and I are fighting back tears as we try not to notice the empty seat beside us. There was going to be no friendly rivalry tonight; no counter-cheering for "spite"; no playful hits and warnings to be quiet.

The Moose Jaw Warriors have had such a disappointing season and, when you look around the stadium, you see all these upset, frustrated fans at times. I would hear angry words and threats of never coming back here because all they do is lose. Some people feel like they are wasting their time.

By contrast, for a life lesson, I need only look to my right and to witness Ron and Eleanor, giggling and laughing the whole time because one was playfully pitted against the other. They were showing me what really matters.

Ron did take a moment later in the game to reflect with us about his life with Eleanor. "We went to so many places over 55 years," He said, "And, it wasn't perfect! There were times we wanted to kill each other. But, who doesn't have that?" He laughed and looked into the distance with a bright smile. He was recalling all the happy times.

That was the thing; he never made it seem more than it was. And, he never made it seem less than it was. He simply made it what it was.

"We had four kids, grandkids and now, a great grandkid," he said, smiling and nodding at his true accomplishments, "I have no regrets."

My mom and I sat there quietly while, on the ice, the game was playing. He saw both my mom and I tear up and he sat back, pointed a scolding finger at us, and says, *"DON'T YOU EVEN START! DON'T EVEN!"*

This was a man who suffered a devastating loss not two days ago. But, like the fighting spirit that needs to live in all of us, he chose life. He would not stand to see us shed a tear or be sad. His tears had been shed in private before coming here and, this was not the time or the place to express sorrow. There was a game going on, afterall!

I would catch myself looking over at Ron over the course of the game. There was many a time he wasn't watching the game and, instead, he chose to watch the tips of his fingers touch each other as if it were a daydream. He was set apart from the moment; he was living between worlds.

That's what you do when loved one passes; you are here, and then you are not.

Ron had his knees replaced years ago – by the way, he says *never* do that! – and for every game, Eleanor would dote on him to make sure he could get into and out of his seat. He said many times that "Eleanor is my legs". Seeing him sit there, alone, with an empty seat between us made me think of who his legs are now; figuratively and literally.

The loss, for me – an acquaintance at best – was starting to settle in. Eleanor was gone and it was palpable. I knew my experience was but a spoonful of an ocean of loss he was feeling. No matter the brave face one wears after a loss, the hole that it leaves in one's life will always surface, if even for a moment.

Remember how Ron always cheered for the visiting teams just to "spite" Eleanor? This night, I gave him a menacing finger point when Prince Albert scored and, I said, "Are you cheering for them?" He laughed, smiled, and said I'd find out. When Moose Jaw scored and, eventually won the game, I saw him clap and cheer. My mom and I looked over at him.

He put a hush finger to his lips and said, "That was for Eleanor".

☙

www.ingramcontent.com/pod-product-compliance
Lightning Source LLC
Chambersburg PA
CBHW061648040426
42446CB00010B/1640